Trust In Leaders and IT Project Success

Rashid Khan

Abstract

The purpose of this quantitative correlational predictive study was to examine if, and to what extent, trust in leaders mediates the relationship between servant leadership and IT project success dimensions of project management success, perception success, and result success within technology project teams in the United States. The study was grounded in the servant leadership theory (Liden et al., 2015), the trust-in-leaders model (Podsakoff et al., 1990), and the IT project success model (Harwardt, 2018). A total of 142 IT project team members in the United States participated in the study. The research utilized validated Likert-scale instruments to assess servant leadership, trust in leaders, and IT project success dimensions. Data were analyzed using the Hayes (2018) PROCESS macro v4.3 in SPSS v29 to test mediation effects via ordinary least squares regression. Results indicated that trust in leaders partially mediated the relationship between servant leadership and IT project success dimensions. The indirect effect of trust in leaders was significant for project management success (β = .149, 95% CI [.032, .264]), perception success (β = .193, 95% CI [.028, .347]), and result success (β = .184, 95% CI [.047, .317]). These findings contribute to the understanding of IT project leadership by demonstrating that trust in leaders enhances the positive effects of servant leadership on project success. The study provides practical implications for IT project management, suggesting that organizations can improve project outcomes by fostering leadership behaviors that build trust within team.

Keywords: Servant leadership, trust in leaders, IT project success, project management success, perception success, result success, perception success, result success, mediation analysis

Table of Contents

Chapter 1: Introduction to the Study

Introduction

One of the most pressing issues in business today is the high failure rates of IT projects, expressing the need for research into effective leadership strategies that mitigate these failures. Moreover, understanding the factors contributing to IT project success and failure is a critical and pressing issue (Schmidt, 2022), with more than 52% of IT projects failing to deliver on the intended short-term benefits. These short-term failures include not meeting the planned budget, scope, and schedule. Across all project life-cycle dimensions, nearly 83.9% of global IT projects fail in whole or in part (Standish Group International, 2019). These failures cost firms billions of dollars worldwide (Schmidt, 2022). However, since the advent of COVID-19, the IT project failure rate has been more than 60% in the United States (L. Ali et al., 2023). According to Schmidt (2022), these IT project failures impose significant financial losses that highlight the urgency of developing practical project leadership approaches and improving team performance. Therefore, this study explored the potential impact of servant leadership strategies on reducing high IT project failure rates.

Over the last decade, servant leadership has been a practical approach to success in projects. However, more current book has found that servant leadership positively impacts IT projects and their related dimensions (Harwardt, 2020). Recent research has identified a need for a better understanding of the relationship between servant leadership and project success, particularly in the IT industry and across different geographical populations. Current research focuses on how the relationship between servant leadership and project success is explained through various moderating and mediating variables, such as interpersonal trust (Mozammel & Abdulla, 2024; Nauman et al., 2023) and trust in leaders (Hassan et al., 2021; Jan, 2025), none of which have been conducted in the IT industry or within the United States. The following paragraphs briefly give an overview of the current book on these geographical and industry trends and developments. This overview is imperative to understanding the problem space and the need for this study.

Current research trends indicate that scholars from various business sectors focus on common issues, particularly the indirect effects that contribute to the success of IT projects under servant leadership. Nauman et al. (2022a) conducted a study on various project types in Pakistan and reported that servant leadership fosters a collaborative culture, which enhances project success through improved team performance. Malik et al. (2022) examined non-governmental organizations (NGOs) in Pakistan and discovered that servant leadership influences project success through emotional intelligence, further bolstered by team effectiveness. Nauman et al. (2022b) found that servant leadership significantly affects project success by reducing project work withdrawal and increasing work engagement in Pakistani vocational training firms. Moreover, Ellahi et al. (2022) conducted a study on software project teams in Pakistan and found that servant leadership positively impacts project success when mediated by team motivation and effectiveness. Additionally, Nauman et al. (2023) explored the effects of servant leadership on project success in the Pakistani construction sector, finding that interpersonal trust mediates, and project governance moderates this relationship. These trends suggest a positive impact of servant leadership on project success across various business sectors and geographical locations.

Additionally, the only research that looked at the relationship between servant leadership and IT project success is by Harwardt (2020), which showed a significant positive impact in German-speaking countries. In 2020, Harwardt highlighted the positive correlation between servant leadership and the success of IT projects and further suggested that future research explore mediating factors such as trust. These trends provide gaps in the book that reveal a lack of research concerning the IT industry in the United States and emphasize the importance of assessing the indirect relationship of trust within this problem space. To further assist in understanding the problem space, reviewing gaps in the current book concerning geographical and industry trends and how they frame this research is imperative.

This study is essential as it contributed to the body of knowledge by addressing several significant gaps. For instance, it bridged the practical knowledge gap (Nauman et al., 2022b) by providing a deeper understanding of the human side of project management. This research also filled the industry and population gaps by examining the

IT industry (Nauman et al., 2023) in the United States (Ellahi et al., 2022; Jan, 2025). Furthermore, it addressed the theoretical gap (Malik et al., 2022) by exploring the mediating role of trust in leaders (Nauman et al., 2022a), which also tied to the methodological-contextual gap. In addition to filling these gaps, this research addressed ways to advance knowledge and business practices.

This study addressed practical and theoretical ways to improve the success of IT projects with followers' trust in their servant leaders. Organizations can develop comprehensive leadership training programs that emphasize enhancing servant leadership behaviors. This can help cultivate leaders who foster trust (Hassan et al., 2021) and collaboration (Ahmadzai, 2024) within their teams, which leads to higher project success rates and reduces financial losses. Additionally, implementing team-building activities that further promote a collaborative culture (Ahmadzai, 2024), innovative work behavior (S. Ali et al., 2023), and work engagement (Nauman et al., 2022b) can enhance the effectiveness of servant leadership. These activities can help team members feel more connected and committed to their projects and improve overall performance. Therefore, the purpose of this quantitative correlational predictive study was to examine if, or to what extent, trust in leaders mediates the relationship between servant leadership and IT project success dimensions of project management success, perception success, and result success within technology project teams in the United States.

Background of the Study

Over the past several decades, the topic of servant leadership and project success has evolved significantly. Early research by Turner and Müller (2005) and Anantatmula (2010) laid the groundwork for understanding practical leadership approaches in project management, identifying the leadership style of project managers as a significant factor in project success. Gwaya et al. (2014) were the first to examine and discover that servant leadership played a role in project success when used in project management. Krog and Govender (2015) found that project leaders with servant leadership traits, such as altruistic calling and emotional healing, positively affect the project team's innovative behavior, commitment, and trust through perceived empowerment. Harwardt (2020) conducted a seminal study that was the first to examine the effects of servant leadership behaviors on IT project success dimensions. Since then, contemporary book has expanded to explore various mediating and moderating factors that help explain the relationship between servant leadership and IT project success.

Building on these significant historical findings, current book has identified various mediating and moderating factors that help explain, strengthen, or weaken the relationship between servant leadership and project success. For example, team effectiveness strengthens the relationship between servant leadership and project success in a study on NGOs (Malik et al., 2022). Additionally, regarding research within NGOs, servant leadership has been found to impact project success through emotional intelligence

(Malik et al., 2022), collaborative culture (Ahmadzai, 2024), team climate, and team identity (Mombeuil et al., 2023). Moreover, studies have also focused on the effects of servant leadership and project success in the construction industry. These findings showed that the relationship between servant leadership and project success was mediated by team cohesion (Khalil et al., 2025), innovative work behavior, psychological empowerment (Ali et al., 2023), interpersonal trust (Mozammel & Abdulla, 2024; Nauman et al., 2023), and trust in leadership (Hassan et al., 2021; Jan, 2025). Another study examined a public vocational training firm and found that servant leadership directly affects project success through project work withdrawal and work engagement (Nauman et al., 2022b). Ellahi et al. (2022) also conducted a study regarding servant leadership impacts on project success in a software development company and found that team motivation and team effectiveness significantly mediate the relationship.

Furthermore, the majority of these studies are conducted in Pakistan (S. Ali et al., 2023; Bilal et al., 2021; Ellahi et al., 2022; Hassan et al., 2021; Malik et al., 2022; Nauman et al., 2023; Nauman et al., 2022a; Nauman et al., 2022b), Afghanistan (Ahmadzai, 2024), The Gaza Strip (Amuna et al., 2021), Indonesia (Little & Martens, 2024), Bahrain

(Mozammel & Abdulla, 2024), and a five-continent study (Mombeuil et al., 2023).

What was not yet known was the application of a more humanistic

(Nauman et al., 2022b) view of the IT sector project management dynamics (Nauman et al., 2023) while also increasing generalizability (Ellahi et al., 2022; Jan, 2025). Although trust factors, including trust in leaders as mediating variables, have been completed in the construction industry (Jan 2025; Nauman et al., 2023), there were still calls to employ further mediating factors (Malik et al., 2022), and specifically trust (Harwardt, 2020), and trust in leaders (Nauman et al., 2022a). While most of this research has been concentrated in Pakistan, no research within the IT industry had been conducted in the United States. Moreover, no studies have explored indirect effects on the relationship between servant leadership and IT project success. Therefore, this research addressed whether trust in leaders mediates the relationship between servant leadership and IT project success dimensions among technology project team members in the United States. This study highlighted the urgent need for effective leadership strategies to enhance project success, as evidenced by the high failure rates of IT projects in the United States, exceeding 60% since 2020 (S. Ali et al., 2023; Schmidt, 2022). This study focused on the IT industry in the United States and contributes to a more profound understanding of utilizing the servant leadership approach to improve project outcomes.

The findings of this study have significant professional and organizational implications, including the potential to enhance leadership training programs, improve IT project success rates, reduce financial losses, and promote team performance. First, servant leadership pushes others to become successful leaders who can serve, providing a positive work culture that promotes task completion (Bilal et al., 2021). Secondly, this study could profoundly influence Human Resources departments through enhancements to training and development programs for leadership (Gu & Liu, 2022). Enhancing trust in leaders can foster a service culture (Hu & Liden, 2011; Liden et al., 2015), which may produce better team performance (Nauman et al., 2022a). Lastly, teamwork quality has a 28.5% influence on the success of projects (Hayat et al., 2022), and these projects provide higher net value for investors (Zwikael & Meredith, 2021). This ultimately leads to improved project success rates and reduced financial loss, crucial factors affecting contemporary business (Schmidt, 2022). Therefore, this research addressed the extent to which trust in leaders mediates the relationship between servant leadership and IT project success dimensions of project management success, perception success, and result success within technology project teams in the United States.

Definition of Terms

The terms in this section contain empirically based conceptual and operational definitions of important constructs, theories, and variables used in this study.

IT Project Success. Harwardt (2020) conceptualizes IT project success (ITPS) as achieving project objectives regarding effective project management, stakeholder perspectives, and financially and strategically measurable business outcomes. The ITPS model includes three subdomains:

short-term, medium-term, and long-term views of IT project success. The subdomains of project management success, perception success, and result success will be measured individually as ordinals approximated to intervals (Norman, 2010). For this study, there were no composite scores for IT project success, and each subscale will be used individually within separate research questions and hypotheses.

Mediation. Mediation is a process in quantitative research where the effect of an intervening variable helps explain the relationship between a predictor variable and a criterion variable (Hayes, 2018). A mediating variable, or mediator, helps researchers understand how the relationship between the independent and dependent variables is explained (Igartua & Hayes, 2021). The mediation variable in this study is trust in leaders. It was used to determine 'how' servant leadership affects the IT project success dimensions of project management success, perception success, and result success.

Organizational Citizenship Behavior. Organizational citizenship behavior, or OCB, is "discretionary contributions or discretionary, unsolicited behavior from members by the organization that employs them" (Sumarmi & Tjahjono, 2021, p. 1). For this study, OCB refers to voluntary employee actions to achieve the organization's goals and improve team effectiveness (Podsakoff & MacKenzie, 1997). In project settings, these discretionary OCB behaviors are known as project citizenship behavior (PCB) and are used interchangeably in this study.

Perception Success. Perception success is the medium-term view of IT project success that evaluates the success of IT projects, including the perceptions of stakeholders, clients, end-users, and team members (Harwardt, 2020). This subscale is ordinal approximated to interval (Norman, 2010). For this study, the dimension of perception success measures medium-term view of IT projects based primarily on team members' perceptions. This subscale included three questions measured as ordinal approximated to interval (Norman, 2010).

Project Management Success. Project management success is the short-term view of IT project success. It examines project success by accounting for benefits that emerge from the planning through execution phases of projects, including meeting the requirements, milestones, schedule, and budget (Harwardt, 2020). For this study, this subscale assessed the immediate project management benefits of successful IT projects, using two questions measured as ordinal approximated to interval (Norman, 2010).

Result Success. Result success is the long-term view of IT project success. Result success assesses the long-term benefits to organizations (Harwardt, 2020). The long-term benefits of IT projects include increased financial performance and the ability to meet the firms' strategic objectives (Harwardt, 2020). This subscale of IT project success is measured ordinal approximated to interval (Norman, 2010). In this research, the result success dimension evaluated the long-term organizational benefits of successful IT projects.

Servant Leadership. The servant leadership model by Liden et al. (2008) conceptualizes an approach to leadership that focuses on serving others, putting their followers' needs ahead of their own, and helping them grow and succeed. This servant leadership model (Liden et al., 2008, 2015) measures seven dimensions of servant leadership behaviors, which will be combined into a single composite score. In this study, the shortened version of the servant leadership model by Liden et al. (2015), the SL-7, was used to determine the direct impacts on the three IT project success dimensions and in the indirect effects on trust in leaders on each of the dimensions of IT project success. This model used seven questions measured as ordinal approximated to interval (Norman, 2010).

Trust in Leaders. Trust in leaders is conceptually defined as reflecting the faith and devotion of employees to the respective leader (Podsakoff et al., 1990). In this study, the trust in leaders model used six questions measured as ordinal approximated to interval (Norman, 2010) that assess the faith and loyalty of project team members toward their project leaders using the servant leadership approach.

Anticipated Limitations

The anticipated limitations in each study regard the weaknesses in the study design, models, theories, or sampling methods outside the researcher's control (Theofanidis & Fountouki, 2018). The following are limitations for this research:

1. This research is cross-sectional, meaning it collects data from a single point in time using a single survey and does not consider changes or observations over a longer period (Cowell, 2020). Therefore, this cross-sectional study limits its generalizability.

2. The study has a quantitative correlational design. According to Theofanidis and Fountouki (2018), this correlational design does not necessarily determine causality. For instance, Queirós et al. (2017) note that correlations found in a study do not "indicate causation because the association between two variables could potentially be explained by a third variable" (p. 382). This limitation will not allow the research to determine causality even if a significant correlational relationship exists between variables.

3. This study uses convenience sampling, another anticipated limitation of the study. Convenience sampling is due to the researcher's proximity to the sampling frame and ease of obtaining the required sample size (Casteel & Bridier, 2021). Although this makes obtaining the optimal sample size more accessible and costeffective, this sampling approach can limit the generalizability of the findings (Emerson, 2021). This impact on external validity is because the sample might not represent the larger population due to a lack of randomization and diversity (Casteel & Bridier, 2021).

4. This study uses a secondary collection approach, volunteer sampling, a type of convenience sampling. Casteel and Bridier (2021) further note that this type of sampling threatens the study's external validity as it is closely related to selfselection bias. Using the volunteer sampling approach, this self-selection bias means that participants may volunteer even though they do not meet the inclusion criteria for the study, potentially skewing the findings.
5. This limitation comes after using convenience and volunteer sampling limitations, as the study uses surveys that collect self-reported data, which can introduce response bias. Response bias is the inclination to provide less than accurate or honest answers, potentially due to the study design, instruments used, or other dynamics (Ming et al., 2021). This limitation can impact internal and external validity due to overreporting or underrepresenting data. This means that the participants could meet the inclusion criteria but are less than honest in their responses, leading to inaccurate results.

6. Another limitation of this study is the use of small, or singledimensional scales. This study employs three criterion subscales with only two measurement items each. Using single or limited measures to assess a given construct can lead to an incomplete or biased understanding of that construct, resulting in monooperational bias (Ferguson, 2004). This limitation can negatively impact the study's external validity and potentially limit its generalizability

(Ferguson, 2004). Additionally, having few items in a measurement scale can reduce reliability, as the scale may not adequately capture the construct across different populations, further impacting generalizability and increasing sampling errors (Kasirye, 2021). Therefore, using only short-form scales for the criterion variables in this study could negatively affect the validity and reliability of the study and limit its generalizability.

Summary and Organization of the Remainder of the Study

Alignment Table

This section provides insights into the study's alignment from the problem space, methodology, design, research questions, hypotheses, and included variables. Table 1 shows the current proper alignment for all study aspects. The alignment was reviewed consistently to ensure no misalignment occurred during the book process. Committee members were a part of the alignment process and approved each process prior to moving to any further relevant stages.

Table 1

Alignment Table

	AlignmentItem Description
Alignment Item	
Problem Space Need:	Current book recommendations have shown that the topic of servant leadership and IT project success is minimal. Therefore, more research on this predictive relationship using social and humanistic perspectives through mediation variables using IT project teams in the United States is needed.
Problem Statement:	It is not known if, or to what extent, trust in leaders mediates the relationship between servant leadership and IT project success dimensions of project management success, perception success, and result success within technology project teams.
Purpose of the Study:	The purpose of this quantitative correlational predictive study is to examine if, or to what extent, trust in leaders mediates the relationship between servant leadership and IT project success dimensions of project management success, perception success, and result success within technology project teams in the United States.

Variables:	Predictor variable: Servant leadership, measured ordinal approximated to interval. Mediator variable: Trust in Leaders, measured ordinal approximated to interval. Criterion variable: Project management success, measured ordinal approximated to interval. Criterion variable: Perception success, measured ordinal approximated to interval. Criterion variable: Result success, measured ordinal approximated to interval.
Research Questions:	RQ1: Does trust in leaders mediate the relationship between servant leadership and project management success? RQ2: Does trust in leaders mediate the relationship between servant leadership and perception success? RQ3: Does trust in leaders mediate the relationship between servant leadership and result success?
Methodology/Research Design Design:	Quantitative Methodology/Correlational-Predictive

---

Summary of Feasibility and Benefits

This study was highly feasible with minimal risk. Several sampling strategies were utilized in parallel. First, initial clearance to use the Project Management Institute (PMI) was approved. However, the PMI Director needed an official IRB document from Grand Canyon University through the researcher to allow access to the email distribution list. There was a clear plan for communicating and obtaining this population.

Additionally, as a secondary research sampling strategy, social media groups were used to ensure a large and diverse population for the sample. The benefits of the survey included a more significant understanding of how servant leadership impacts IT project success through followers' trust. The findings could assist businesses in improving or creating robust leadership training programs. The data collection process was streamlined and required no more than 10 minutes from each participant, minimizing any risk of exhaustion. Moreover, due to the multiple strategies, there was a high number of potential participants, and this study was completed within a reasonable timeframe with minimal risks.

Chapter Summary and Organization of the Remainder of the Study

In summary, the chapter shows a critical issue of high failure rates in IT projects, with over 52% failing to deliver short-term benefits and nearly 83.9% failing in whole or globally (Schmidt, 2022; Standish Group International, 2019). The COVID-19 pandemic has exacerbated this issue, pushing the failure rate to over 60% in the United States (L. Ali et al., 2023). These failures cause significant financial losses, emphasizing the need for effective leadership strategies to improve team performance and project outcomes. The purpose of this study was to examine whether, and to what extent, trust in leaders mediates the relationship between servant leadership and IT project success, particularly focusing on the IT industry within the United States.

The background of the study also discussed that servant leadership has been shown to positively impact project success across various sectors and geographical locations, including NGOs, construction, vocational organizations, and software development companies (Nauman et al., 2022a; Malik et al., 2022; Nauman et al., 2022b; Ellahi et al., 2022). However, there is a notable gap in research explicitly examining the IT industry in the United States. The study fills this gap by investigating how trust in leaders mediates the relationship between servant leadership and IT project success dimensions, such as project management success, perception success, and result success. This research contributes to the body of knowledge by providing insights into effective leadership strategies that can enhance IT project outcomes and reduce financial losses.

The remainder of the study will be organized as follows: the current book regarding how trust in leaders potentially mediates the relationship between servant leadership and IT project success dimensions with be presented in Chapter 2. The book review focuses on empirical research regarding the broad variable topics and then lead to the current book regarding the interplay between variables. Chapter 3 described the justification of methodology, design, and analysis procedures for this study. Chapter 4 provides a detailed written and graphical description of the analysis of the study's findings. Lastly, Chapter 5 summarizes the findings, discusses the implications, and offers recommendations for future research.

Chapter 2: Book Review

Introduction to the Chapter and Background to the Problem

This quantitative correlational predictive study examined if trust in leaders mediates the relationship between servant leadership and the IT project success dimensions of project management success, perception success, and result success using a population of IT project team members within the United States. This study surveyed IT project team members regarding their trust in servant-leading project managers. IT project team members' perspectives influenced three dimensions of IT project success. Ultimately, this study addressed the theoretical and practical business insights to improve IT project outcomes through effective servant leadership as explained by their followers'

trust.

The keywords used for this study included servant leaders*, trust in leader*, follower' trust, project management success, project success, IT project success, IT project management success, project outcomes, IT project outcomes, project effectiveness, IT project effectiveness, project performance, and IT project performance. Combinational phrases were also used, for example: "servant leadership impacts on project success," "servant leadership and trust in leaders," "trust in leaders and project management success," and "servant leadership and project success and trust in leaders." In addition to Google Scholar, additional Grand Canyon University library databases were used for this search, including EBSCOhost, ProQuest, JSTOR, Emerald Insight, ScienceDirect, Web of Science, and PsycINFO.

Information was retrieved from these articles, peer-reviewed journals, conference notes, book chapters, and other materials.

Additionally, Hayes (2018) was purchased and reviewed to better understand statistical regression models, specifically model 4 for mediation, discussed further in Chapter 3. Most cited materials come from peer-reviewed empirical articles published within the last five years.

This book review chapter contains six sections and several other subsections. The first is the background of the problem, which provides a broad overview of the problem space, its brief evolution, and the problem statement for this study. Second, is the identification of the problem space, which provides a more detailed overview of the historical evolution and development of the problem space, including the creation of the problem statement from what has yet to be known in the book. The theoretical foundations section will examine the history and development of the theories and models used for this study: servant leadership theory, the trust in leaders model, and the IT project success model.

The fourth and most comprehensive section is the book review, which introduces and provides critical insights into the history of each of the main variables and insights into the fundamental studies and research on the interconnectedness of the variables from research published in the last five years contains eight sections. The book review begins with three broad sections: servant leadership's impact on individuals, organizations, and team dynamics. Specifically, the servant leadership section will look at how this leadership approach impacts discretionary work behaviors, known as Organizational Citizenship Behavior (OCB), and team-level outcomes. The second broad section encompasses trust in leaders and how trustworthiness is gained by competent, benevolent leaders who possess integrity (Kim et al., 2004; Mayer et al., 1995). These leadership behaviors positively influence their trustworthiness as perceived by their followers. This perception is known as trust in leaders and has positive outcomes, like team- (Cai et al., 2023) and organizationallevel performance improvements (Mai et al., 2023). The third broad section comprises the IT project success and related dimensions. The IT project success section will include subsections on the short-, medium-, and longterm views of IT project success, along with an overview of other relevant models with comprehensive views of project success.

The last five sections of the book review include the interrelated variables and the current book regarding how they have been empirically researched. The fourth overall section is about servant leadership's impact on trust in leaders. The fifth section concerns the effects of trust in leaders on project success. Moreover, the sixth section regards the influence of servant leadership on project success, which effectively shows most of the boundaries of the current book for this study. The seventh section contains comprehensive book discussing the mediating role of trust in leaders in the current book space. Lastly, the eighth section provides a view into the most related research in terms of this study, the impacts of servant leadership on project success when mediated by trust dynamics.

This chapter identifies the problem space and develops the problem statement across several sections. Additionally, presenting the current state of the book regarding each study variable provides a more holistic understanding of the topic and interrelated topics. This section will close out with a summary and introduce Chapter 3, which includes the rationale for methodology and design, hypotheses, instrumentation, and data collection and analysis procedures.

Background to the Problem

The broad historical evolution shows that early research on this topic concerned determining the most appropriate leadership style for completing projects (Anantatmula, 2010; Geoghegan & Dulewicz, 2008; Jiang, 2014; Turner & Müller, 2005). However, the next evolution explored the servant leadership approach, which improved the success of construction projects (Gwaya et al., 2014). In comparison, limited contemporary research has found that servant leadership behaviors positively affected IT project dimensions (Harwardt, 2020). Therefore, what is known is that servant leadership impacts project success, with a focus on NGOs (Ahmadzai, 2024; Amuna et al., 2021; Little & Martens, 2024; Malik et al., 2022; Mombeuil et al., 2023) and construction (S. Ali et al., 2023; Hassan et al., 2021; Jan, 2025; Khalil et al., 2025; Mozammel & Abdulla, 2024; Nauman et al., 2023). Most of the studies were conducted in Pakistan (S. Ali et al., 2023; Bilal et al., 2021; Ellahi et al., 2022; Malik et al., 2022; Nauman et al., 2023; Nauman et al., 2022a; Nauman et al., 2022b). Although a single study was carried out in the United States, it was within the NGO industry (Mombeuil et al., 2023), displaying a lack of research regarding the IT industry within the United States. Additionally, much of the research has focused on the indirect effects of this relationship. Four studies examined servant leadership's impacts on project success through trust (Hassan et al., 2021; Jan, 2025; Mozammel & Abdulla, 2024; Nauman et al., 2023). However, they were also conducted using Pakistani construction projects, leaving significant gaps in the book regarding the IT industry in the United States.

Thus, it had not yet been determined how servant leadership affects the success of IT projects in the United States. Identifying the factors contributing to IT project success should be a topic of current research in the United States and improving servant leadership internationally. There were also no mediated variables related to the relationship, the population, or the industry in the United States. These indirect variables are called out in the book as being a need (Malik et al., 2022), such as trust aspects (Harwardt, 2020), and specifically trust in leaders (Jan, 2025; Nauman et al., 2022a). Thus, this specific research calls for an exploration of to what extent trust in leaders mediates the relationship between servant leadership and the IT project success dimensions of project management success, perception success, and result success within

IT project teams.

Identification of the Problem Space

Existing research highlights gaps in understanding the relationship between servant leadership and project success, particularly across industries and geographical populations. Fourteen significant studies were reviewed to identify the problem space for this research, with six framing it. These studies focus on servant leadership and project success, mediating and moderating variables within various regions and industries. These studies offer a comprehensive book overview, highlighting gaps and support from similar studies by Hassan et al. (2021), Jan (2025), Mozammel and Abdulla (2024), and Nauman et al. (2023), that need expansion into different industries and geographical locations. The remaining relevant studies will assist in strengthening the problem space framework. Subsequent paragraphs will detail current trends in servant leadership and project success.

Current research trends show that researchers from different business sectors are addressing common issues, such as understanding the indirect variables contributing to project success under servant leadership. These trends suggest a positive impact of servant leadership on project success across various sectors, including NGOs (Ahmadzai, 2024; Amuna et al., 2021; Little & Martens, 2024; Malik et al., 2022; Mombeuil et al., 2023), construction (S. Ali et al., 2023; Hassan et al., 2021; Jan, 2025; Khalil et al., 2025; Mozammel & Abdulla, 2024; Nauman et al., 2023), vocational organizations (Nauman et al., 2022b), general projects (Nauman et al.,

2022a), and software development companies (Bilal et al., 2021; Ellahi et al., 2022). These studies were conducted in diverse geographical settings, including Pakistan (S. Ali et al., 2023; Bilal et al., 2021; Ellahi et al., 2022; Hassan et al., 2021; Malik et al., 2022; Nauman et al., 2023; Nauman et al., 2022a; Nauman et al., 2022b), Afghanistan (Ahmadzai, 2024), The Gaza Strip (Amuna et al., 2021), Indonesia (Little & Martens, 2024), Bahrain (Mozammel & Abdulla, 2024), and a five-continent study (Mombeuil et al., 2023). This synbook highlights a need for more research on the IT industry in the United States and underscores the importance of understanding indirect relationships to identify the problem space further.

Current book shows various mechanisms explaining the relationship between project success and servant leadership. Servant leadership focuses on followers' needs, creating a supportive environment that enhances project teams' effectiveness and clarifies team processes and goals (Bilal et al., 2021). Servant leaders promote a collaborative culture (Ahmadzai, 2024) that endorses psychological empowerment and innovative work (S. Ali et al., 2023), thereby improving project success (Nauman et al., 2022a). They also enhance team cohesion (Khalil et al., 2025), team motivation, team effectiveness (Ellahi et al., 2022), team climate, team identity (Mombeuil et al., 2023), and emotional intelligence (Malik et al., 2022). Moreover, servant leadership mitigates employee project work withdrawal more effectively than encourages work engagement (Nauman et al., 2022b). Successful projects are influenced by servant leaders who enhance mutual trust (Nauman et al.,

2023) and develop the perceived trust of their followers (Hassan et al., 2021; Jan, 2025). Additionally, only one study reviewed the success of IT projects in German-speaking countries with a single mediating variable recommendation for utilizing trust (Harwardt, 2020). These studies suggest that servant leadership significantly impacts project success across industries globally and provide recommendations for future research that assist in framing the problem space further.

Future research recommendations and limitations help identify gaps and construct the problem space. Nauman et al. (2022b) recommended expanding into other project contexts conducive to servant leadership from the human project management perspective. Several studies emphasize understanding the mechanisms explaining the relationship between servant leadership and project success through additional mediating and moderating variables (Malik et al., 2022), such as trust in leaders (Jan, 2025; Nauman et al., 2022a). Nauman et al. (2023) noted that future studies need to expand the understanding of project management dynamics by examining the IT industry. Further recommendations suggest exploring different locales, as these studies could be more generalizable (Ellahi et al., 2022; Jan, 2025). Synthesizing these future research recommendations integrates several gaps into parameters that justify the problem statement.

Using what is known and what is not known can help develop a problem space and lead to a practical problem statement. Many studies on servant leadership and project success have been conducted in Pakistan (S.

Ali et al., 2023; Bilal et al., 2021; Ellahi et al., 2022; Malik et al., 2022; Nauman et al., 2023; Nauman et al., 2022a; Nauman et al., 2022b), with the majority involving the construction (S. Ali et al., 2023; Hassan et al., 2021; Jan, 2025; Khalil et al., 2025; Mozammel & Abdulla, 2024; Nauman et al., 2023) and NGO sectors (Ahmadzai, 2024; Amuna et al., 2021; Little & Martens, 2024; Malik et al., 2022; Mombeuil et al., 2023). This leads to recommendations for research in different regions (Ellahi et al., 2022), in the western context (Jan, 2025), and expanding into the human side of project management (Nauman et al., 2022b) within the IT industry (Nauman et al., 2023). While requests for additional mediating and moderating variables (Malik et al., 2022) continue to dominate the book with quantitative correlational studies, one such mediating variable recommended was trust in leaders (Nauman et al., 2022a), conducted prior to that recommendation but in the construction industry with varying instruments in Pakistan (Hassan et al., 2021). In conclusion, further synbook of what is known and not known highlights the need for understanding how trust in leaders mediates the relationship between servant leadership and the IT project success dimensions in technology project teams within the United States, which this study aims to effectively answer.

This study incorporates these recommendations and contributes to the body of knowledge by examining the human side of project management to address the practical knowledge gap (Nauman et al., 2022b), the industry gap (Nauman et al., 2023) through examining the IT industry, the theoretical gap

(Malik et al., 2022) by a mediating variable, such as trust in leaders (Nauman et al., 2022a), which ties to the methodological-contextual gap. Lastly, this study expands research into the United States, effectively addressing a population gap (Ellahi et al., 2022; Jan, 2025) within the current book.

Several potential professional and organizational applications could come from this study. One implication is human resource organizational enhancements through training programs for servant leaders (Gu & Liu., 2022). These training programs will promote the development of a supportive work culture that fosters team effectiveness (Bilal et al., 2021), team cohesion (Khalil et al., 2025), innovative work behaviors, and psychological empowerment (S. Ali et al., 2023), which promotes positive team performance (Nauman et al., 2022a). Furthermore, developing trust in leaders through servant leadership can also improve the financial project performance of firms (Hayat et al., 2022). Therefore, this study addressed these current book gaps and contributes to the body of knowledge by providing organizations with recommendations for hiring and training servant leaders. This research could lead to improved project success rates through having trusted leaders guiding IT project teams.

Theoretical Foundations

The foundational structure for this study has three theoretical frameworks or models, which explore the extent to which trust in leaders mediates the relationship between servant leadership and three IT project success dimensions. The first model, the Servant Leadership (SL-7) model by

Liden et al. (2015), is a condensed version of the original (SL-28) model (Liden et al., 2008). This univariate measure of servant leadership identifies seven altruistic behaviors (Haq et al., 2022) in various settings, including business environments. The second model, the Trust-in-Leaders Model (TIL) by

Podsakoff et al. (1990), evaluates the indirect relationship between followers' perceived trust in their leaders and the success of IT projects. This model helps to understand how trust mediates the impact of servant leadership on project outcomes. The third framework is the IT project success (ITPS) model by Harwardt (2018). It examines project outcomes based on perceived benefits across three dimensions: project management success, perception success, and result success. This section will discuss the foundations of these models and their relevance to the research questions. It will conclude by synthesizing these models and justifying their use in this study.

Servant Leadership Theory

The first theoretical foundation is the servant leadership theory, introduced by Robert K. Greenleaf in his article 'The Servant as Leader' (Greenleaf, 1970). This theory aims to positively change society by fostering humble and empathetic leaders (Greenleaf, 1977). Initially, these were just philosophical tenets without a developed model. Since then, seven multidimensional and three one-dimensional models have emerged, each with unique characteristics (Van Dierendonck, 2011). Despite lacking a universally agreedupon definition of servant leadership (Barbuto & Wheeler,

2006; Chughtai, 2016), several prominent operational models have been developed. The three most utilized models, in chronological order, are Ehrhart (2004), Liden et al. (2008), and Van Dierendonck and Nuijten (2011).

For this research, Liden et al.'s (2015) model (SL-7) is the most appropriate foundational concept for utilization. This servant leadership model (SL-7) developed by Liden et al. (2015) is a short-version, global model of the original SL-28 created by Liden et al. (2008). The SL-7 model has been examined in industries such as healthcare (Bibi, 2022), consulting (Lemoine et al., 2023), education, telecommunications (Wang et al., 2021), banking (Zeeshan et al., 2021), service and manufacturing (Kumari et al., 2022), and the IT sector (Khan et al., 2024). For this study, servant leadership is conceptually defined as "placing the needs of their subordinates before their own needs and centering their efforts on helping subordinates grow to reach their maximum potential and achieve optimal organizational and career success" (Liden et al., 2008, p. 163). The SL-7 was utilized in this research as a single global score to calculate the impact on IT project success and trust in leaders, using Liden et al.'s (2008, 2015) seven servant leadership behavioral dimensions of emotional healing, conceptual skills, empowering subordinates, creating value for the community, behaving ethically, helping subordinates grow and succeed, and putting subordinates first. These dimensions collectively form the conceptual model for the SL-7 instrument, which aims to measure the extent to which leaders display servant leadership behaviors. Therefore, this single global score was used to calculate the direct impact of servant leadership on the three dimensions of IT project success and the indirect impact on trust in leaders.

Trust in Leaders Model

The second theoretical foundation is the trust-in-leader model (TIL), which is conceptualized as follower faith and follower loyalty combined to measure the variable of trust in leaders as perceived by their followers or subordinates (Podsakoff et al., 1990). Moreover, for this study, the TIL model uses a single variable to measure overall perceived trust in leaders by their subordinates or followers. This model of trust, created by Podsakoff et al. (1990), was developed from earlier studies using loyalty to the Leader (Giffin, 1967; Rotter, 1967) and interpersonal trust by Cook and Wall (1980). Podsakoff et al. (1990) further developed the interpersonal trust model that used the dimension of faith in leaders, highlighting the followers' viewpoint. Podsakoff et al. (1990) added the second dimension of loyalty in leaders to form the operationalized trust-in-leaders model, which was quickly adopted and widely used in existing book.

According to Podsakoff et al. (1990), trust in leaders conceptually reflects subordinates' faith and devotion to their leaders. This trust-in-leaders model is still broadly utilized as a mediator in business settings. Trust in leaders has been operationalized in business sectors like project-based organizations (Raiz et al., 2023), healthcare (Afshari et al., 2023; Khawar et al., 2023), hotels (Baquero, 2023), banking (Rafiq et al., 2022) and IT and software (Bhatti et al., 2021). These studies show that the trust-in-leader model by Podsakoff et al. (1990) is still relevant and beneficial in today's empirical book. This study uses this trust-in-leaders model to explain the relationship between servant leadership and the three IT project success dimensions.

IT Project Success Model and Dimensions

The third foundational model is the IT project success model (ITPS) developed by Harwardt (2018). This model will be analyzed using three criterion variables conceptualized into three dimensions of project success over three benefit timeframe perspectives: short-, medium-, and long-term success. The short-term view is known as project management success, conceptualized by Harwardt (2018) as ensuring the project's objectives are met regarding time, budget, scope, and resources. The mediumterm view is known as perception success, conceptualized as the end-user or client's perspective on the success of projects (Harwardt, 2018). Moreover, the longterm view of success is known as result success, which is conceptualized as the long-term financial or strategic benefits to a firm (Harwardt, 2018). The ITPS model was developed to address the lack of specific instruments for measuring IT project success from management's perspective (Harwardt, 2018, 2020). A single study was conducted using this model by Harwardt (2020), which comprised participants from German-speaking countries, validating its reliability. However, 44 articles have cited Harwardt's (2020) study on the impacts of servant leadership behaviors and IT project success, indicating its growing recognition in IT industry book.

Summary

These three theoretical frameworks and models help to understand how trust in leaders mediates the relationship between servant leadership and these IT project success dimensions. The theory of servant leadership by Liden et al. (2015) provides altruistic servant behaviors, such as putting others first (Haq et al., 2022), with a rich history in business, including the IT sector (Khan et al., 2024). The trust-in-leaders model (Podsakoff et al., 1990) offers insights into the indirect role of leaders' subordinates, with a history of use in IT (Bhatti et al., 2021) and projectbased industries (Raiz et al., 2023). The IT project success model (Harwardt, 2020) supports the criterion variable by analyzing project success dimensions and understanding IT project benefits over time through a team member lens, aligning with the other two instruments.

Together, these models address the research questions aligned with the problem statement, examining how trust in leaders mediates the relationship between servant leadership and IT project success dimensions among technology project team members. Integrating these models provides insights into the validations of servant leadership, trust in leaders, and IT project success, enhancing their interconnected practical and theoretical understandings within the IT sector. The trust-in-leader model is newly applied to this industry, examining a different population, while the IT project success model proposes greater generalizability through population expansion.

Review of the Book

Introduction

The book review examines the overarching variable and the broad seminal and current book framing this research. Looks at how trust in leaders, directly and indirectly, from the team member perspective, influences the relationship between servant leadership and IT project success dimensions. Furthermore, reviewing the current book will show a gap concerning the IT industry and a need for studies within the United States.

This book review has eight comprehensive sections, with the first three sections providing a broad overview of the overarching variables of servant leadership, trust in leaders, and IT project success dimensions in this study. These three sections present several relevant subthemes regarding team member perceptions concerning their leadership and research regarding leadership behaviors leading to increased perceptions of trust. The five remaining sections explore the current study and assist in framing the gaps in book. Ultimately, these sections will compare the current book for each variable, along with research on the interplay between them. A synbook is provided at the end of each section to help provide the basis and framework for the problem space section following the book review, along with the relevant gaps this study intends to address.

Servant Leadership

The theory of servant leadership and related behaviors is a historically effective tool that creates impactful results for individuals, organizations, and team settings. The concept of servant leadership, a term coined by Robert Greenleaf in his 1970 article 'Servant as Leader' (Greenleaf, 1977), was formed on the behaviors of leaders who choose to serve first and lead second. However, the origins of servant leadership can be traced back to the biblical and philosophical teachings of Jesus Christ and Lao Tzu, for example. The servant behaviors spoken of and practiced by Jesus Christ are found biblically in Matthew 20:20-28, Mark 10:41-45, Luke 22:23-27, and John 13:3-10 (Yengkopiong, 2023, p. 41). The ancient Chinese philosopher Lao Tzu emphasized the importance of kindness in leadership, stating, "Kindness in words creates confidence. Kindness in giving creates love" (Van Dierendonck et al., 2023, p. 306). The teachings and behaviors of these historical figures laid the foundation for the practice of servant leadership, emphasizing the importance of serving others with love and compassion (Greenleaf, 1977). The following paragraphs compare the effectiveness of servant leadership within team settings using organizational citizenship behavior (OCB) and team performance as themes. The themes of OCB and team performance are particularly relevant to this study because they are vital elements of servant leadership's impact on individuals' discretionary work within teams or OCB behaviors, potentially leading to performance improvements for project teams. These will be further integrated and presented in later sections of this book review.

The first theme on the impacts of servant leadership on OCB provides evidence for improving the effectiveness and performance of individuals, organizations (Howladar & Rahman, 2021), and teams (Parris & Peachey, 2013). Organ defines OCB in Podsakoff et al. (2000) as "discretionary individual behavior not formally acknowledged by the reward system and collectively contributes to the organization's efficiency and effectiveness" (p. 513). Although some recent studies have focused on the direct effects of servant leadership on OCB (Haji et al., 2021; Kumari et al., 2022; Mirza et al., 2023), the impact of servant leadership on OCB has been more thoroughly examined indirectly. The positive mediations of OCB involve job embeddedness (Zia et al., 2022), employee self-efficacy (Isabel et al., 2023), job satisfaction (Ngah et al., 2022), relational energy (Özkan et al., 2023), employee engagement (Srimulyani & Hermanto, 2022), emotional intelligence (Kumari et al., 2022), organizational commitment (Howladar & Rahman, 2021), leader-member exchange (LMX), and trust (Anselmus Dami et al., 2024). Additional findings showed that servant leadership enhances team performance through individual-level OCB, team-level internal social capital, and team-member exchange (TMX), providing more evidence that OCB impacts individual, organizational, and team outcomes (Ruiz-Palomino et al., 2023). Extant book indicates that leaders who are servants first promote OCB behaviors since they support employees in taking on additional work outside of their typical roles (Podsakoff et al., 2000). Therefore, servant leaders enhance individual, organizational, and team performance (Ruiz-Palomino et al., 2023) while encouraging employees to take on additional work tasks, like projects. Although these studies offer valuable insights into how servant leadership positively influences employees, firms, and teams through OCB, they are not without criticism.

Servant leadership faces limitations and criticisms despite the positive benefits of OCB within individual, organizational, and team settings. Several studies on the correlation between servant leadership and OCB indicated that servant leadership has no significant effect on OCB (Fira et al., 2023; Sabila & Anshori, 2022; Susanto, 2023). For instance, a study by Sabila and Anshori (2022) found that servant leadership has no significant impact on OCB. This finding suggests that these leaders do not influence employees' discretionary work due to perceptions that the leader provides preferential treatment towards only some employees and not all. Another example of a drawback to servant leadership and OCB is a study by Fira et al. (2023) that inferred no significant effect on OCB or job satisfaction. Individual-level servant leadership is also criticized because it negatively affects OCB through psychological entitlement, especially when there is lower group-mean servant leadership (Si et al., 2023). Although these studies show that servant leadership may encounter situations with no significant impacts, the vast majority unveil that servant leadership fosters an OCB culture, improving individual behaviors and organizational effects. This research helps explain employees' behaviors that can lead them to be embedded into a matrixed project team, as servant leaders are understood to encourage individual discretionary work like projects. The following paragraphs involve the effects of servant leadership on team-level performance within organizations.

Another theme is the current research surrounding team-level performance, which contributes to the effectiveness of servant leadership in organizations. Devine and Philips (2001, p. 512) defined team performance as "the degree to which a team accomplishes its goal or mission." According to Hindiyeh and Cross (2022), the antecedents of team performance are efficiency, effectiveness, and innovation. Additionally, servant leadership improves team performance, promotes collaboration, and encourages knowledge sharing when mediated by team goal clarity, team process clarity, and team knowledge creation (Bilal et al., 2021; Nauman et al., 2022a; Yu et al., 2021). Moreover, Ren and Shen (2024) uncovered that bolstering servant leadership behaviors improves team innovative performance through innovative self-efficacy. Similar studies establish that servant leadership significantly affects team performance through other various mediating mechanisms, such as team cohesion, team learning (Abdolmaleki & Ghanbari, 2021), team climate (Arshad et al., 2022), increased work engagement (Zhou et al., 2022), internal social capital, TMX (Ruiz-Palomino et al., 2023) and teamwork (Swanson et al., 2022). Nauman et al. (2022a) ascertained that, in project-based firms, servant leadership influences team performance through collaborative culture. This research reveals that servant leadership significantly impacts team performance through different mediating and moderating mechanisms. However, not all mediating variables show positive effects, as some result in non-significance or adverse effects on individual and team performance.

The previous paragraphs discuss the generally accepted idea of servant leadership; however, several important opposing mediating factors have adverse effects on the performance or effectiveness of teams. The study by Nauman et al. (2022a) found that while collaborative culture mediates the relationship between servant leadership and project team performance, knowledge sharing does not, which contradicts recent results. Another study found that servant leadership weakens group member performance when the leader-member relationship and the group interrelationships become too polite (Hashmi & Siddiqui, 2023). The current book space concerning servant leadership's impact on performance focuses typically on the individual (Khattak et al., 2023; Zada et al., 2023) or organizational level of performance (Alipio et al., 2023; Ludwikowska & Tworek, 2022). However, these findings illustrate that there is still an open debate, or gap, in understanding the impacts of servant leadership on team performance (Nauman et al., 2022a; Ruiz-Palomino et al., 2023; Yu et al., 2021) and potential adverse team outcomes, such as examination of project success. The remaining paragraphs will discuss and synthesize this gap through these findings and suggestions reviewed in the previous paragraphs.

Understanding OCB and team performance is essential for servant leaders within organizational settings. Mainly because OCB and team performance help form a comprehensive view of servant leadership's effects in organizational team settings. In the context of OCB, the book addresses servant leadership as crucial in encouraging employees to carry out discretionary work (Podsakoff et al., 2000). Moreover, servant leadership impacts OCB directly (Haji et al., 2021; Kumari et al., 2022; Mirza et al., 2023) and indirectly (Anselmus Dami et al., 2024; Howladar & Rahman, 2021; Isabel et al., 2023; Kumari et al., 2022; Ngah et al., 2022; Özkan et al., 2023; Srimulyani & Hermanto, 2022; Zia et al., 2022) through broad factors to promote individual and team performance outcomes (Ruiz-Palomino et al., 2023). As for team performance, the book reflects that servant leadership affects team performance through mediating variables (Abdolmaleki & Ghanbari, 2021; Arshad et al., 2022; Ren & Shen, 2024; RuizPalomino et al., 2023; Swanson et al., 2022; Zhou et al., 2022), along with enhancing project team performance (Bilal et al., 2021; Nauman et al., 2022a; Yu et al., 2021). Therefore, as Nauman et al. (2022a) discovered, OCB and team performance are essential aspects of an organization's team dynamics, including project and individual team member aspects. These team-level factors contribute to this study, focusing on individual contributions to team-level discretionary project work.

Additionally, these themes are significant as they focus on the principles that servant leadership contributes to, such as the discretionary work of employees and innovative team results. Moreover, OCB and team performance are significant factors in the success of project teams and organizations (Nauman et al., 2022a). Although the current servant leadership book provides an understanding of its direct positive impacts on team performance and effectiveness, more research still needs to explore additional mediating factors (Malik et al., 2022), such as trust in leaders (Nauman et al., 2022a), within the information technology industry (Nauman et al., 2023). This study addresses this issue, explicitly referring to the mediating factor of trust in leaders, which is the subject of the ensuing section.

Trust in Leaders

This section examines the trust of leaders and how followers' perceptions of their leader lead to individual, organizational, and team performance. Early trust models discuss bidirectional relationships, which are more general, like interpersonal trust (Rotter, 1967) and organizational trust (Giffin, 1967). Rotter (1967, p. 651) defined interpersonal trust as "the confidence of an individual or collective that a promise in any form made by another individual or collective is reliable and can be expected." However, since interpersonal trust focuses on mutual trust, much of the book lacked the followers' viewpoint on how leaders are trusted (Mishra & Mishra, 2013). The interpersonal trust models (Giffin, 1967; Rotter, 1967) were further developed by Cook and Wall (1980), who introduced the dimensions of faith and confidence in leaders, emphasizing the employee's point of view. Later,

Podsakoff et al. (1990) adopted a new dimension that replaced confidence in leaders with loyalty in leaders and coined the trustin-leaders model. The trust-in-leaders model was quickly adopted and used broadly in extant book.

The trust-in-leaders model includes the dimensions of faith and loyalty in leadership (Podsakoff et al., 1990). The book explains that other leadership behaviors also contribute to followers' perceptions of faith and loyalty in their leaders. These behaviors include reliability, compassion, openness (Mishra & Mishra, 2013), competence, benevolence, integrity (Kim et al., 2004; Mayer et al., 1995), fairness, and honesty (Dirks & Ferrin, 2002). These themes are crucial for team-level outcomes concerning followers' perceptions of their leader (Kim et al., 2004; Mayer et al., 1995). Trustworthy behaviors, as referenced in Farmanesh and Zargar (2021), highlight the characteristics of servant leaders. The following paragraphs will explore how these individual perceptions of leadership behaviors impact interpersonal trust levels within individuals and team members, as well as their relevant outcomes and criticisms.

Integrity. A leader's integrity positively influences individual and team-level performance. Individual employee perceptions of their leaders' integrity are crucial to team performance, commitment, engagement, and organizational success. Additionally, integrity is considered the most influential factor regarding the trustworthiness of a leader (Yan et al., 2023). Holmes and Parker (2017) found that a leader's integrity behaviors positively encourage followers' perceptions when their words and actions are aligned, and following through on their commitments improves reliability, credibility, and trustworthiness. Leaders wanting more effective teams must display greater integrity, meaning they stick to and honor their promises and commitments (Zia-ur-Rehman et al., 2022). Additionally, exploring the impacts of leadership, organizational equity, and integrity on organizational commitment, Sharma and Hans (2022) found that integrity is the most significant factor. Molle et al. (2023) discovered that when employees and team members view their leader as possessing integrity, they are more likely to trust that leader.

Furthermore, greater levels of leadership integrity further enhance credibility and trustworthiness when consistently adhering to their promises (Holmes & Parker, 2017) and honoring their commitments (Zia-ur-Rehman et al., 2022). These follower perceptions foster organizational commitment, engagement, and success (Shabir & Muazzam, 2024; Yan et al., 2023). This theme helps to show how a perceived leader's integrity within team settings can influence the faith and loyalty of followers, which are relevant to Podsakoff et al.'s (1990) trust-in-leaders model. Although integrity is considered the most critical factor (Sharma & Hans, 2022), competency is another essential factor in building trust in leadership, leading to positive team-level outcomes based on followers' perceptions.

Competence. The second trust-in-leaders theme concerns individual team members' perceived competence in their leader concerning their impact on team-related outcomes. Competence, another factor in the formation of trust (Kim et al., 2004; Mayer et al., 1995), is defined by Woodruffe (1993) as "the set of behavior patterns that the incumbent needs to bring to a position to perform its tasks and functions with competence" (p. 29). Moreover, Greenleaf (2007) stated that leaders must display selfconfidence, moral judgment, and competence to cultivate trust.

Arafat and Darmawati (2022) found that job satisfaction is the outcome of competent leadership, arguing that when competence and job satisfaction are combined, individuals are encouraged to perform as a team. Furthermore, empowering and competent leaders promote follower motivation through relational energy, further promoting team performance (Cai et al., 2023). Result-oriented leader competence, product, and process innovations directly impacted organizational performance, emphasizing the connection between perceived leadership competence and team performance (Mai et al., 2023). This book suggests that when perceived as empowering, result-oriented, competent leadership influences job satisfaction and both team and organizational performance through the energy created between employee interactions (Arafat & Darmawati, 2022; Cai et al., 2023; Mai et al., 2023). While perceived competence and integrity are essential for building trust in followers, perceived benevolence is another crucial factor.

Benevolence. The third theme related to followers' perceptions of leaders and enhancing their trust concerning team dynamic outcomes is benevolence. Benevolence puts the well-being and interests of those who work closely together (Schwartz, 1992). Individuals with this value aspire to be "helpful, loyal, forgiving, honest, responsible, true friendship, mature love" (Schwartz, 1992, p. 11). A benevolent leader, therefore, looks after subordinates both in and out of the workplace (Farh et al., 2008) and provides a supportive and safe work setting (Li & Xing, 2021). These values extend to the followers' perceptions of benevolence in their leaders within team settings. As Li and Li (2021) noted, benevolence enhances trust because team members view the leader as not concerned with their self-interests but preferring the team's well-being.

Additional findings show that a combination of leaders' power and benevolence values, especially when benevolence is high, predicts positive follower-focused leadership and outcomes, such as satisfaction and nurturing behavior (Sverdlik et al., 2022). Shen et al. (2023) found that benevolent leaders are strengthened in a trusting environment, improving job performance when explained through harmonious passion. This research shows a significant relationship between benevolence, employee performance, and the need for a trusting work setting. Moreover, leaders develop trustworthiness when followers perceive them as possessing integrity, competence, and benevolence (Farmanesh & Zargar, 2021; Kim et al., 2004; Mayer et al., 1995). While book shows positive perceptions of trust, there appear to be some situations where trust may not be as beneficial.

Summary. Trust in leaders can be less favorable to organizational and teambased outcomes, provided certain conditions. For instance, trusting overconfident leaders harms procedural and interpersonal justice on the business's financial performance (Bonau, 2022), meaning that overconfident leaders may overlook fairness when taking on financial risks. As noted by Moore (2021), "Overconfident leaders put themselves, their teams, and their organizations at risk" (p. 58). Another example is when applying authoritarian leadership approaches, a leader's trust can be outweighed by the adverse effects on the social exchanges between leaders and their followers, possibly harming team and organizational outcomes (Farmanesh & Zargar, 2021). Moreover, from the followers' viewpoint, when pairing trust in leaders with the dark triad personality traits of narcissistic leaders, the leadermember exchange (LMX) and team performance are degraded, suggesting that trust in leader outcomes may not promote performance (Fodor et al., 2021). The positive and negative aspects of developing trust in leaders conclude that confidence, integrity, and benevolence are significant positive factors, while overconfidence is one of the major potential detractors. The following paragraphs will synthesize the themes presented in this section.

The trust-in-leaders model conceptualizes followers' faith and loyalty in their leadership. This model provides an understanding of the individual perceptions of follower trust to foster organizational and team performance. In developing trust, leaders must display trustworthiness, influencing followers' perceptions of their integrity, competence, and benevolence (Farmanesh & Zargar, 2021; Kim et al., 2004; Mayer et al.,

1995). When followers view their leader as having integrity, it improves their trustworthiness by being reliable and credible, leading to team and organizational success
(Holmes & Parker, 2017; Shabir & Muazzam, 2024; Zia-ur-Rehman et al., 2022). Perceived leader competence promotes trust by displaying empowering and resultoriented leadership qualities, improving job satisfaction and task performance, along with organizational and team performance (Arafat & Darmawati, 2022; Cai et al., 2023; Greenleaf, 2007; Mai et al., 2023). Benevolent leaders promote trust and team performance by putting the needs, interests, and well-being of the team members ahead of their own (Farh et al., 2008; Li & Li, 2021; Li & Xing, 2021; Schwartz, 1992; Shen et al., 2023; Sverdlik et al., 2022).

In contrast, a loss in followers' trust in leadership happens when leaders are overconfident, authoritarian, or display dark triad traits, leading to negative organizational and team performance (Bonau, 2022; Farmanesh & Zargar, 2021; Fodor et al., 2021; Moore, 2021). These studies were selected as they took employees' perceptions and how that perception impacts trust in their leaders. This viewpoint is how the trust in the leader's variable will be examined in the study, making this an appropriate framework. Additionally, they present a gap in the book regarding the lack of mediating factors in team settings, explicitly looking at IT project team dynamics (Malik et al., 2022; Nauman et al., 2023). The following paragraphs will discuss the factors of IT project success in more detail.

IT Project Success

There are several different IT project success models in the book today. However, only one model has been developed and operationalized using the management's perspective (Harwardt, 2018, 2020). Early success factor models included clear goals, project team commitment, funding, team capability, cost estimation, planning and controls, and task orientation (Baker et al., 1997). However, as De Wit (1988) noted, it was only at the Project Management Institute (PMI) conference in Montreal in 1986 that it focused on measuring project success based on progress, cost, and quality. Several others were produced in the following years (De Wit, 1988; Pinto & Slevin, 1987) with a focus on relevant factors such as project mission, management support, scheduling, personnel, monitoring, communication, and client acceptance, to name a few.

However, the most widely used criteria for project success are the iron triangle, which involves evaluating projects based on whether they are completed within budget and on time with the correct implementation of requirements (Atkinson, 1999), which widely regards the traditional criteria for evaluating the success of projects (Shenhar et al., 2001). However, the iron triangle only shows temporary benefits (Collins & Baccarini, 2004) through evaluations of the project management life cycle (Müller & Turner, 2007). These factors, however, do not fit all project types, and controversy splits project success into two factions: traditional project success models and IT/information security (IS) project success models. The following will delve into IT/IS project success models' background, current use, and limitations.

This disagreement in the success criteria and factors led Baker et al. (1997) to explain that there is only partial success when it comes to project management and that the evaluation of projects should happen over time. It continues to be an issue today in both traditional and IT projects. This divergence between criteria based on project type started in 1992 with DeLone and McLean's (D&M) Model (DeLone & McLean, 2003), which looked at the benefits to information security dimensions of information quality, quality of the system, and service quality that can impact system usage, and user satisfaction (Harwardt, 2020). Wateridge (1995) was one of the first to review overall project performance and quality; it also included perspectives of customers and endusers.

Recent developments in models of IT project success assess this multidimensional aspect of success (Müller & Turner, 2007). The basis of these dimensions in the book views the time frames that measure the success benefits in short-, medium- and long-term views (Harwardt, 2020; Joseph & Marnewick, 2021). The following paragraphs discuss each of these views on the success continuum, where current research is regarding them and their unique impacts, with a final discussion on the relevant models that have a holistic view of the success continuum and where they converge and diverge with each other, finally leading into the model by Harwardt (2018, 2020) and why it is relevant to this study.

Short-Term Success View. The short-term view is the most prevalent criterion in the book regarding project success. This short-term view is commonly known as the Iron Triangle or the triple constraint (Baccarini, 1999), focuses on schedule variances, budget, and scope (Atkinson, 1999) and can also include resource management efficiency and quality (Joseph & Marnewick, 2021). Later, Cooke-Davies (2002) introduced the current project management success terminology, replacing the old Iron Triangle convention. Short-term success criteria link to project management success (Baccarini,

1999) and project efficiency (Shenhar et al., 1997), which is the short-term success (Harwardt, 2018) criterion variable for this study.

Proper project planning is the crucial process that leads to short-term project success or failure. Ardika and Nurmala (2021) learned that schedule variances come from problems in the analysis stage. These issues lead to project delays and increased costs and negative impact on the success of the IT project (Ardika & Nurmala, 2021). Additional risks to project failure include poor project scope definitions, inadequate planning, and inaccurate estimations, leading to incongruent goals (Allam & Akre, 2021; Althiyabi & Qureshi, 2021; Hamid et al., 2022; Kotowaroo & Sungkur, 2022). Whereas deficient planning can cause project failures, proper planning can improve the success of projects.

In contrast to insufficient planning, proper planning, and transparent scope requirements can impact project success outcomes through enhanced control, mitigating scope creep, and relevant objectives (Kotowaroo & Sungkur, 2022). Short-term success is obtained through proper planning and clear scope definitions (Kotowaroo & Sungkur, 2022). At the same time, projects fail due to issues in the analysis stage (Ardika & Nurmala, 2021) and poor project scope definitions, inadequate planning, and incorrect estimations (Allam & Akre, 2021; Althiyabi & Qureshi, 2021; Hamid et al., 2022; Kotowaroo & Sungkur, 2022). This research on IT project success explains that the iron triangle, or triple constraint, is still relevant today.

The short-term success criteria, known historically as The Iron Triangle, are intrinsically linked to project management success (Joseph & Marnewick, 2021). The success or failure of an IT project depends on its schedule, scope, and budget (Ardika & Nurmala, 2021) or the triple constraint criteria (Baccarini, 1999). While The Iron Triangle, or project management success in this study, is still used in assessing project success, it is considered the least impactful on the IT project success time scale (Harwardt, 2018, 2020). The following section will discuss the medium-term success criteria, or perception success, which include the perceptions of clients, stakeholders, team members, and end-users.

Medium-Term Success View. In contrast to the short-term view, medium-term success takes a broader view, considering the internal and external perspectives of various stakeholders involved in a project (Harwardt, 2018; Wateridge, 1995). This research uses the medium-term view of success as 'perception success' (Harwardt, 2018, 2020). This broad view of IT project success looks at the perspectives of clients, team members, stakeholders, and end users (Davis, 2014; Harwardt, 2020). The following paragraphs examine these broad perspectives and their impact on the success of IT projects.

The perspectives of all stakeholders are relevant concerning the medium-term view of project success, known here as perception success (Harwardt, 2018). To improve the client's satisfaction and project success, project leadership must align the client's requirements with the project type (Woźniak, 2021). Moreover, the satisfaction of the end-user perspective promotes project value perceptions and overall success through feedback, integrating the end-user requests and benefits into the project design process (Surma-aho et al., 2022). Another factor in project success is the ability of managers to apply clear objectives through a democratic approach, allowing team members to make decisions, which, according to research by Kotowaroo and Sungkur (2022), is perceived as a significant factor by more than 70% of team member respondents (p. 12). Stakeholder engagement and communication through effective stakeholder management is also a contributing factor as it enhances the probability of success of projects by mitigating risks, aligning stakeholder expectations, and facilitating contingency strategies (Figueiredo Filho et al., 2022). However, failure to apply these stakeholders to these strategies can impair the success of projects.

Project leaders must ensure attainable objectives, defined scope, user involvement, and communication management to mitigate project failures. From the client's perspective, Kotowaroo and Sungkur (2022) determined that the main reasons for IT project failures are unrealistic objectives and a lack of defined goals. From the team members' viewpoint, the authors also found that failure rationales were due to a lack of user involvement and an undefined scope (Kotowaroo & Sungkur, 2022). An additional study by Jasmi et al. (2022) found that division between top management support and middle management negatively impacts project effectiveness, emphasizing better communication between middle and upper management.

The influences on the medium-term view of IT project success are a complex concept looking at the perspectives of clients, team members, stakeholders, and endusers. This medium-term perspective fosters satisfaction, integrates feedback into the design process, applies clear objectives, and provides effective engagement and communication to enhance project outcomes (Figueiredo Filho et al., 2022; Kotowaroo & Sungkur, 2022; Surma-aho et al., 2022; Woźniak, 2021). Additionally, unclear objectives, undefined scope, and lack of user involvement and stakeholder communications can diminish the success of IT projects (Jasmi et al., 2022; Kotowaroo & Sungkur, 2022).

Therefore, the short- and medium-term view discussion on IT project success provides insights into project management and perception success. Meanwhile, the medium-term view or perception of success (Harwardt, 2018) includes the perspectives of clients, end-users, stakeholders, and team members. This study focuses primarily on the project team members' perspectives, potentially limiting the results of this success dimension. The following section will provide an overview of the financial and organizational impacts that comprise the long-term view of IT project success.

Long-Term Success View. Although short- and medium-term IT project success views are essential, this study's ultimate measure of an IT project's success is its longterm impact or net benefits (DeLone & McLean, 2003). Moreover, this research's longterm view is termed the 'result success' dimension (Harwardt, 2018, 2020). This 'result success' dimension includes financial benefits, such as operating income and strategic advantages providing a competitive edge (Harwardt, 2018, 2020). Shenhar et al.'s (2001) original idea for an IT project success continuum argued that the long-term success dimension includes project benefits that produce organizational benefits over the longterm perspective. Therefore, dimensionality is considered a controversial measure.

Farbey et al. (1992) are difficult to assess, as the actual results of a project can deviate significantly from the intended outcomes and benefits achieved as part of a project in the long term. Finally, the suggested model by

Harwardt (2018) can view each time frame comparison by the project team members working on the IT projects with different measures of success, thus removing the necessity for new target measurements or benchmarks (Thomas & Fernández, 2008). The following paragraphs assess recent studies about IT project success's long-term financial and organizational impacts.

The long-term view of IT project success offers various financial, strategic, and organizational advantages. Several primary financial metrics of productive IT project success evaluation for businesses are cost savings and revenue generation (Jasmi et al., 2022). However, to be fully realized over time, IT project success must include strategic advantages, business value, and organizational benefits. Ensuring that IT projects align with the overall business strategies improve organizational performance and creates a strategic competitive advantage (Andry, 2023). Another significant long-term IT project success view is that of business value, as the expectation of IT investments is to promote performance outcomes (Pashutan et al., 2022), like process and capability improvements of organizations, which may materialize those results months or years after completion of the IT project (Reich & Peppard, 2022). Zaleski and Michalski (2021) stated that several benefits of successful IT projects include improvements in organizational agility, sustainability, and stakeholder engagement. These authors infer that engaging and aligning with stakeholders is essential due to the challenges in measuring longer-term intangible project benefits and is necessary to avoid governance failures and ensure accountability.

The long-term view of IT project success is also complicated, with broad benefits ranging from financial, strategic, and organizational aspects that typically appear over a longer time frame (Reich & Peppard, 2022). These generated benefits include cost savings, revenue generation (Jasmi et al., 2022), competitive advantage (Andry, 2023), performance enhancements (Pashutan et al., 2022; Reich & Peppard, 2022), increased agility, greater sustainability, and improved stakeholder engagement (Perera et al., 2023; Zaleski & Michalski, 2021). The research regarding the long-term view provides insights into the complexities and benefits that make up project success over a longer time frame. While the previous subsections discuss the dimensions and how they benefit businesses over each period, some models provide a multidimensional view incorporating all time frames.

Multidimensional Success Models. This subsection compares four relevant IT/information security (IS) project success models, considering an aggregate view of the unique criteria factors along the IT project success continuum. While there has yet to be a consensus on the project success construct, researchers agree it is a multidimensional measurement (Atkinson, 1999; Basten et al., 2011; De Wit, 1988; Shenhar et al., 1997). The model by DeLone and McLean (2003) was created to comprehensively assess projects from the perspective of information system effectiveness and their impacts on businesses using the IS projects' six dimensions: system quality, information quality, service quality, use, user satisfaction, and net benefits. In comparison, Shenhar et al. (2001) designed the diamond model from the strategic project management perspective with the four dimensions of project efficiency, customer impact, business success, and future potential. This diamond model views outcomes based on short- and long-term stakeholder perspectives (Shenhar et al., 2001). Zwikael and Meredith (2021) also a holistic model for evaluating project success through academics, industry experts, and business executives. This model uses the dimensions of project management success, project ownership success, and project investment success. The last model by Harwardt (2018) is the first and only current framework for evaluating IT project success as formed from the management perspective using the dimensions of project management success, perception success, and result success.

While all these models can successfully evaluate IT project success, only one is particularly relevant to this study. The model by DeLone and McLean (2003) focuses on information system quality and usage, making it the least suitable of the four instruments for this study. The diamond model evolved from the strategic project management viewpoint (Shenhar et al., 2001). Due to the unique traits of each project, Shenhar et al. (2001) using different dimensions based on the unique project type. In comparison, Zwikael and Meredith (2021) designed a model of project success that was more generic and better suited for this study as it incorporates views from academics, industry experts, and business executives.

In contrast, the ITPS model has been developed based on interviews across management levels, including 21 team leaders and middle and senior managers involved in IT project analysis (Harwardt, 2018). The model was operationalized using the management's perspective in a study comprised of 646 project leaders, project managers, Scrum Masters, and executives in the IT industry (Harwardt, 2018). Since this study collected data from the IT project team members and management perspectives, the ITPS model was the most appropriate. Summarizing each perspective provides insights into each time frame on the success continuum of short-, medium-, and long-term views that will come next.

Summary. In conclusion, the IT project success book depicts a complex and evolving environment with various interpretations and models of success criteria over the years. The project success models initially stressed the importance of well-defined objectives, a dedicated team, and accurate cost estimation (Baker et al., 1997). Others suggested evaluating success based on progress, cost, and quality (De Wit, 1988). This progress led to the creation of the Iron Triangle, which uses short-term success criteria of budget, time, and scope (Ardika & Nurmala, 2021; Atkinson, 1999). However, Baker et al. (1997) note that the Iron Triangle is limited since it needs a long-term dimension.

In response to these limitations, multidimensional frameworks were developed (Müller & Turner, 2007) to integrate short-term (Iron Triangle), medium-term, and longterm perspectives into comprehensive models (Harwardt, 2020; Joseph & Marnewick, 2021). While the short- and mediumterm views are essential, the long-term views provide the most significant benefits (DeLone & McLean, 2003; Harwardt, 2018, 2020). The long-term view of success evaluates the net benefits of projects over time (DeLone & McLean, 2003). These long-term benefits include cost savings (Jasmi et al., 2022), promoting competitive advantage (Andry, 2023), enhancements of organizational capabilities (Pashutan et al., 2022), and improved sustainability (Zaleski & Michalski, 2021). However, assessing projects with a single view introduces limitations in research.

Therefore, multidimensional models were created to ascertain each study's benefits. Several of these models focus on information systems (DeLone & McLean, 2003) and generic models that include IT projects (Shenhar et al., 2001; Zwikael & Meredith, 2021). However, the ITPS by Harwardt (2018) was the most capable model for this study as it assesses the management's perspective of IT project success over various periods. Furthermore, this model helped address the gap in understanding the human side of project management (Nauman et al., 2022b), such as exploring the relationship between servant leadership and IT project success dimensions through trust in leaders as a potential mediator.

Servant Leadership and Trust in Leaders

Servant leaders promote employee well-being and development directly and indirectly through trust in leaders. This section explores servant leadership, its impact on followers' trust, and the resulting organizational outcomes within the current book. Servant leaders prioritize the well-being and growth of their followers and exhibit altruism, integrity, and humility (Haq et al., 2022), promoting positive interactions that create a work environment of trust and increased work engagement (Rahal & Farmanesh, 2022).

Additionally, trustworthy servant leaders were found to strengthen employee engagement (Zhou et al., 2022). Moreover, servant leaders look after their followers' development, needs, empowerment, and skills; this enhances trust in their leader and selfefficacy (Brohi et al., 2021; Iqbal et al., 2021). Divya (2022) demonstrated that authentic servant leadership improves followers' trust and reduces employee burnout. Another study uncovered that servant leaders who remain objective improve followers' trust while motivating employees and increasing customer satisfaction (Qiu & Dooley, 2022). While servant leadership enhances followers' trust in previous studies, there are circumstances where trust in leadership diminishes.

Although these studies suggest that servant leaders positively impact followers' trust, commitment, and self-efficacy, servant leadership has a dark side that can hinder these effects, including trust. Servant leaders who have followers with increased Machiavellian behaviors experience psychological entitlement, leading to deviant behaviors, especially when their leader gives weak, negative feedback. (Gao & Liu, 2023). Another recent study shows that in a selfish attempt to benefit the leader or business, use of the servant leadership approach may unintentionally increase unethical behaviors among employees (Uymaz & Arslan, 2022). Zheng et al. (2024) found that wellbeing and trust can be damaged when servant leaders experience exhaustion due to increased follower job demands and resources. Despite these challenges, servant leadership generally promotes positive results for followers and organizations.

The servant leadership approach improves follower trust and promotes positive business outcomes. Likewise, trust is a significant component of servant leadership (Greenleaf, 1977). Servant leaders foster an environment of support (Qiu & Dooley, 2022; Zhou et al., 2022) through altruistic behaviors, integrity, and humility (Haq et al., 2022). Moreover, servant leaders look out for their followers' well-being, growth, needs, skills, and empowerment (Brohi et al., 2021), which enhances trust in their leader. Furthermore, servant leadership fosters employee engagement (Zhou et al., 2022), work engagement (Rahal & Farmanesh, 2022), follower self-efficacy (Iqbal et al., 2021), and reducing employee burnout (Divya, 2022). Therefore, fostering followers' trust in their servant leaders does promote positive individual and organizational outcomes. However, limited studies have assessed servant leadership and follower trust influences within IT project teams, highlighting the current gap and recommendations for this study (Nauman et al., 2023). The following section of this book review will discuss trust in leaders and the impacts on the success and performance of projects and project teams.

Trust in Leaders and Project Success

This section provides insights into how trust in leaders affects project performance. The research on this topic, although limited, is entirely relevant to this study. Trust in leaders positively impacts project success by enhancing team performance, communication, collaboration, and coordination. Trust improves team performance and project success by promoting positive team interactions (Chuang et al., 2021). Zhang and Li (2024) posited that the project manager's competency level directly impacts project performance and indirectly through employee trust, communication, capability, and team atmosphere. A study by Fareed et al. (2022) revealed that transformational leaders should foster team trust and job satisfaction to promote successful projects. These studies express that trust in leaders influences project success directly and indirectly. Leadership styles like transformational and ethical approaches can further enhance project success, displaying this section's particular relevance for this study.

Similarly, understanding the positive impacts of follower trust and performance can also be evaluated by looking at the effects of distrust. For instance, employees may feel ability-distrusted when they have a competent leader, resulting in diminished work effort and job performance (Lu et al., 2021). This distrust leads to poor performance, lower self-efficacy, and decreased work effort. Li et al. (2023) also observed that project performance, collaboration, and cooperation suffer due to asymmetric trust between project owners and their partners. Furthermore, business trust decays due to losing trust between followers and team members. This loss of trust leads to employee disengagement, increased turnover rates, stress, and other mental health issues within teams (Hungerford & Cleary, 2021). Hungerford and Cleary (2021) further noted that team members can improve their workplace through the behaviors of "benevolence, competence, reliability, honesty, vulnerability, and openness" (p. 512). Understanding what trust and distrust behaviors affect is vital for mitigating potential negative impacts while enhancing work performance for employees and team members.

This research shows that team members and leaders can help improve their business environments and build follower trust within their teams. These positive findings of trust in leaders suggest it improves project success (Bhatti et al., 2021; Majeed et al., 2021), team performance (Chuang et al., 2021), job satisfaction (Fareed et al., 2022), and project performance (Zhang & Li, 2024). Positive project outcomes are particularly effective when fostering trust using transformational (Fareed et al., 2022), authentic (Majeed et al., 2021), and ethical leadership approaches (Bhatti et al., 2021). Conversely, distrust can have adverse effects like poor project performance (Li et al., 2023), decreased job self-efficacy (Lu et al., 2021), knowledge hiding (Kadam & Kareem Abdul, 2024), and employee disengagement (Hungerford & Cleary, 2021).

Therefore, leaders must foster trust in their followers. This implies that servant leadership should do the same since transformational and ethical leadership styles can improve project success. Conducting more studies while examining IT project settings can address this gap in book. The following section will review servant leadership's impact on project success.

Servant Leadership and Project Success

The current book regarding servant leadership's impact on project success is limited, especially in the context of IT project success. This section discusses these limited studies concerning the location, organizational type, sample size, and findings. Delving into the current book with this focus will help reveal the gaps surrounding the limited IT project success research while additionally showing the need for more servant leadership correlations with IT project success research in the United States (Nauman et al., 2023).

Highlighting these gaps helps the understanding of the potential for substantial contributions to the management and business fields by exploring these relationships in different contexts and industries. Many studies regarding servant leadership and general project success are centered in Pakistan (S. Ali et al., 2023; Ellahi et al., 2022; Hassan et al., 2021; Malik et al., 2022; Nauman et al., 2023; Nauman et al., 2022a; Nauman et al., 2022b). These are all correlational predictive studies that primarily involve nongovernmental organizations (NGOs) (Ahmadzai, 2024; Amuna et al., 2021; Malik et al., 2022; Mombeuil et al., 2023) or construction firms (S. Ali et al., 2023; Jan, 2025; Khalil et al., 2025; Nauman et al., 2023). One additional study by Harwardt (2020) was conducted in German-speaking countries. It found a positive relationship between servant leadership behaviors and IT project success while highlighting the need to examine the relationship with trust as a mediator. Expanding into several of these studies will highlight the need to add IT project success research in the United States to the current book.

Malik et al. (2022) examined the mediation effects of emotional intelligence and job stress and the moderation effects of team effectiveness on the relationship between servant leadership and project success. The study included 441 project team members from an NGO in Pakistan. The results, using partial least square structural equation modeling (PLS-SEM), indicated that servant leadership had a positive effect on project success ($\beta = 0.16$, $t = 2.72$, $p = 0.007$) and emotional intelligence ($\beta = 0.38$, $t = 8.475$, $p < 0.001$) (Malik et al., 2022). These findings indicate that servant leaders may enhance project success in part through emotional intelligence. Malik et al. (2022) also found that servant leadership had no significant indirect impact on project success through job stress. This study revealed that team effectiveness enhanced the relationship between servant leadership and project success (Malik et al., 2022). In contrast, the negative impact of job stress was diminished in the presence of team effectiveness, while team effectiveness had no significant effect on the impact of emotional intelligence on project success (Malik et al., 2022). Ultimately, businesses promoting servant leadership and fostering team effectiveness can help the success of projects.

Additionally, some studies involve more than a single NGO. For instance, Ahmadzai (2024) conducted a study that included multiple NGOs within Kabul, Afghanistan. This study explored the relationship between servant leadership and project success and the mediation effects of collaborative culture using surveys gathered from 230 NGO employees (Ahmadzai, 2024). Results of the study, using Hayes's (2018) model 4 PROCESS macro, show that servant leadership has a highly significant impact on the success of projects ($\beta = 0.7164$, $t = 16.6248$, $p < 0.001$) (Ahmadzai, 2024). Ahmadzai (2024) also found that collaborative culture significantly correlated with project success and mediates the relationship between servant leadership and project success. This relationship highlights the importance of servant leaders instilling an environment of collaboration within project teams to enhance project outcomes in NGOs.

These findings coincide with the earlier research by Malik et al. (2022) of NGOs in

Pakistan. However, research reveals similar outcomes in more broadly sampled studies.

Limitations to previous research on NGOs are that they view only specific geographical locations, which hinders their generalizability. For example, Mombeuil et al. (2023) empirically analyzed the relationship between servant leadership and project success and the mediating roles of team identity and team climate. The study survey was disseminated over five months to 25 NGOs in each country of Africa, Asia, Europe, Latin America, and the United States for a total of 125 NGOs and 451 valid responses (Mombeuil et al., 2023). The 451 respondents were divided into two groups of employees and volunteers to examine the study's intended results on different NGO stakeholders. The results of the study found, using the Hayes

(2018) PROCESS macro in SPSS, that between all groups, there was a positive significant impact of servant leadership on project success (β = 0.2420, $t = 6.3521$, $p < 0.001$), team climate (β = 0.6781, $t = 22.0657$, $p < 0.001$), and team identity (β = 0.5567, $t = 16.5519$, $p < 0.001$) (Mombeuil et al., 2023).

Moreover, team climate and team identity positively mediated the relationship between servant leadership and project success (Mombeuil et al., 2023). The analysis also showed that servant leadership and project success were stronger for volunteers (β = 0.325) than for employees (β = 0.094) and that the effects of team climate on project success were more significant for employees (β = 0.483) than for volunteers (β = 0.136) in NGOs (Mombeuil et al., 2023). The research here assists servant leaders in approaching stakeholders differently, as each has a unique impact on the success of projects and feelings of being part of the team. Promoting team identity for employees and volunteers can improve the success of projects in NGOs globally.

Research by Nauman et al. (2022b) examined the mediating impacts of work engagement and project work withdrawal and the moderating factor of project identification on the relationship between servant leadership and project success. This research comprised 453 project team leader-member dyads over two time periods collected from a large public vocational training firm in Pakistan (Nauman et al., 2022b). Findings from Nauman et al. (2022b), using PLS-SEM and Hayes (2018) PROCESS macro for mediation in SPSS, show that there is a direct effect of servant leadership and project success ($\beta = 0.174$, $t = 4.821$, $p < 0.001$) and is indirectly explained through project work withdrawal ($\beta = 0.095$, $t = 4.416$, $p < 0.001$) and work engagement ($\beta = 0.125$, $t = 5.396$, $p < 0.001$). However, work withdrawal has a more significant indirect explanation of project success than work engagement (Nauman et al., 2022b). These findings suggest that servant leaders can help enhance project success by improving employee work engagement and mitigating work withdrawal behaviors. While the findings are positive for NGOs and vocational organizations, research also shows that servant leadership assists in construction projects.

Another study by S. Ali et al. (2023) investigated the relationship between servant leadership and project success and the mediating effects of innovative work behavior and psychological empowerment on that relationship. The study received 350 valid survey responses from construction industry professionals in Islamabad, Pakistan (S. Ali et al., 2023). Results from the structural equation modeling and Hayes (2018) PROCESS macro for SPSS showed that servant leadership explained variances in each variable: 60.9% of project success, 54.7% % of psychological empowerment, and 24.4% of innovative work behavior (S. Ali et al., 2023, p. 2162). Furthermore, S. Ali et al. (2023) found that servant leadership has a significantly positive impact on project success ($\beta = 0.22$, $t = 3.538$, $p = 0.000$), and using Hayes mediation (Hayes, 2018) that innovative work behavior ($\beta = 0.133$, $t = 3.855$, $p = 0.000$) and psychological empowerment ($\beta = 0.273$, $t = 3.933$, $p =$

0.000) mediate the relationship between servant leadership and project success. Therefore, servant leaders who foster innovative work and empower their project team members contribute to project success within construction settings in Pakistan.

A study by Khalil et al. (2025) investigated the relationship between servant leadership and project success and the mediating effects of team cohesion and the moderating effect of top management support. The study captured 476 survey responses from construction industry professionals and project managers in Pakistan (Khalil et al., 2025). Results from the structural equation modeling showed that servant leadership had a positive significant impact on project success ($\beta = 0.291$, $t = 4.410$, $p < .001$) (Khalil et al., 2025). Moreover, Khalil et al. (2025) found that servant leadership has a significantly positive effect on project success mediated by team cohesion ($\beta = 0.149$, $p < .001$, 95% CI [0.091, 0.220]) and further moderated by top management support ($\beta = 0.334$, $t = 8.146$, $p < .001$). Therefore, servant leaders who promote team cohesion can improve the success of construction projects, while additionally strengthening this relationship by gaining top management support. This research completes the relevant findings in the construction industry, however, there is one that presents findings for the IT industry.

The last study is the only one that considers the information technology sector, specifically the software development market. Ellahi et al. (2022) researched the mediating impacts of team motivation and team effectiveness on the relationship between servant leadership and project success. The study comprised 219 software development team members employed in software development organizations within Pakistan (Ellahi et al., 2022). Calculating the results using SPSS and the Hayes (2018) model 4 PROCESS macro for mediation and parallel mediation shows that the direct effect relationship between servant leadership and project success was significant ($\beta = .264$, SE = 0.0787, CI [0.1097, 0.4199], $p < .01$) (Ellahi et al., 2022). Moreover, the variables of team motivation ($\beta = .310$, SE = 0.0731, CI [0.1505, 0.3921], $p < .01$) and team effectiveness ($\beta = .244$, SE = 0.0685, CI [0.1095, 0.3797], $p < .01$) are significant positive mediators in the relationship between servant leadership and project success (Ellahi et al., 2022). This study by Ellahi et al. (2022) highlights the importance of providing empowerment, motivation, and team development to improve the successful outcomes of projects within the software development industry.

These studies emphasize the current field of servant leadership and project management and the mechanisms for understanding their effects on project success. The findings in these studies show the significance of servant leadership behaviors in the project management field and how they impact the success of projects in NGOs (Ahmadzai, 2024; Amuna et al., 2021; Malik et al., 2022; Mombeuil et al., 2023), construction firms (S. Ali et al., 2023; Jan, 2025; Khalil et al., 2025; Nauman et al., 2023), vocational organizations (Nauman et al., 2022b) and software development (Ellahi et al., 2022) in various regions around the globe. However, these studies were primarily explored in Pakistan (S. Ali et al., 2023; Ellahi et al., 2022; Hassan et al., 2021; Malik et al., 2022; Nauman et al., 2023; Nauman et al., 2022b), only one had a small aspect that involved the United States (Mombeuil et al., 2023). Moreover, only one study delved into a minor element of information technology projects, however, did not use an IT project success model in its analysis (Ellahi et al., 2022). Therefore, there are no current studies involve the United States and information technology organizations or project team members.

Additionally, explanations of these project outcomes, when in the presence of the servant leadership approach, are through collaborative culture (Ahmadzai, 2024), team identity, team climate (Mombeuil et al., 2023), team cohesion (Khalil et al., 2025), work engagement (Nauman et al., 2022b), innovative work behavior, psychological empowerment (S. Ali et al., 2023) intelligence (Malik et al., 2022), team motivation and team effectiveness (Ellahi et al., 2022). These findings highlight the need to explore other mediating tools that can help explain project success in the context of servant leadership, which is the gap this study intends to address. One potential mediator used extensively in current and historical studies is trust in leaders, which the following section will discuss.

The Mediating Role of Trust in Leaders

This section examines the current book on trust in leaders as a mediator. According to Hayes (2018), the simple mediation model is the most basic form of a mediation model. Hayes (2018, p. 78) defines it as a “statistical method used to evaluate evidence from studies designed to test hypotheses about how some causal antecedent variable *X* transmits its effect on a consequent variable *Y*.” In simple terms, this definition means that the mediator variable indirectly affects the relationship between the independent (predictor) variable and the dependent (criterion) variable, explaining how the relationship occurs (Igartua & Hayes, 2021). The following paragraphs will review the current research on servant leadership as the predictor variable and its direct outcomes through trust in leaders. Subsequently, it will explore how these predictor variables impact project success through trust in leaders. The following section will discuss various leadership styles that influence project success through trust in leaders.

The current book reflects that interpersonal bi-directional trust and trust in leaders influence project success through different leadership styles. Research findings indicate that transformational leadership positively influences project success through trust and job satisfaction, and further strengthened by emotional intelligence (Fareed et al., 2022; Saeed et al., 2023). Additional research indicates that ethical leadership impacts project success through trust in the leader and knowledge sharing (Bhatti et al., 2021). Humble leadership also positively affects project success through employee commitment to the project (Hassan et al., 2023). In contrast, Khan et al. (2021) noted that transformational leadership is less influential than laissez-faire or transactional leadership when mediated through trust. Khan et al. (2021) also iterated that transformational leadership had no significant impact on project success. Furthermore, interpersonal and follower trust help to explain these relationships.

The following section will delve into the outcomes associated with servant leadership and the indirect mediating effects of trust in leaders, as highlighted in current book. The current research has various outcomes, many of which can partially explain followers' trust in their leadership, which more closely aligns with this study.

Kadarusman and Bunyamin (2021) found that servant leadership impacts job performance through trust in leaders and knowledge sharing, meaning employees who trust their leaders are more willing to share knowledge and enhance their performance. A study by Anselmus Dami et al. (2024) found that servant leadership has a significantly positive effect on job satisfaction through trust in the leader and leader-member exchange (LMX) and that servant leadership has a significant impact on organizational citizenship behavior via trust in the leader and leader-member exchange (LMX). In research by Putri et al. (2023), job satisfaction uncovered that servant leadership positively influences job satisfaction through trust in leaders. Additionally, Luo's (2022) results show that servant leadership influences employees' innovative behavior through trust in leaders.

Regardless of leadership style, when leaders feel mentally or emotionally depleted, it can negatively impact performance, leading to a lack of trust and fewer citizenship behaviors (Haesevoets et al., 2022). Therefore, when the servant leadership approach is utilized, trust in leaders indirectly

impacts outcomes such as job performance (Kadarusman & Bunyamin, 2021), job satisfaction (Anselmus Dami et al., 2024), organizational citizenship behavior (Putri et al., 2023), and employee innovative behavior (Luo, 2022), while also ensuring that they are not emotionally or mentally exhausted
(Haesevoets et al., 2022).

Moreover, ethical (Bhatti et al., 2021), humble (Hassan et al., 2023), transformational (Fareed et al., 2022; Saeed et al., 2023), transactional, and laissez-faire leadership (Khan et al., 2021) styles indirectly impact project success through trust in leaders. Overall, the consensus of current research displays the impacts of trust in leaders and interpersonal trust on project success, especially when in the presence of servant leaders. The following section will discuss the current research regarding the aggregation of servant leadership and project success when mediated by trust and provide insights into the gap in book this study aims to inform regarding examining the IT sector, which is currently a gap in book.

Servant Leadership, Trust in Leaders, and Project Success

This final section of the book review will discuss the four studies, which are most like this study. These studies will comprehensively compare methodology, design, instrumentation, sample size, and industry. This analysis will compare the topical nuances in the extant book and further frame the gaps this study intends to address. Only three studies have examined how interpersonal trust or trust in leaders mediates the relationship between servant leadership and project success. However, no study has utilized these variables to explore the IT industry until this study. The following paragraphs will review these three empirical studies in order of relevance to this research.

The first study is a correlational predictive study by Nauman et al. (2023) that examined when and how servant leadership fosters success in construction megaprojects and whether interpersonal trust mediates, and project governance moderates this relationship. The sample comprised 273 construction project managers and team members (Nauman et al., 2023) in Pakistan. Results used linear regression to show the positive direct impact of servant leadership on project success ($\beta = .4481$, $p < 0.001$) (Nauman et al., 2023). Additionally, Hayes's (2018) PROCESS macro Model 4 for SPSS was used to test for the mediation of interpersonal trust, in which the direct effect of servant leadership on project success was positive and significant ($\beta = .4481$, $t = 8.3421$, $p < 0.001$), the indirect effect was significant ($\beta = .2315$, $t = 3.5937$, $p < .001$), and interpersonal trust positively mediated ($\beta = .2166$, SE = 0.0517, CI [0.1194, 0.3232], $p < .05$) (Nauman et al., 2023). Moreover, interpersonal trust was found to be more significant when there are lower levels of project governance and weaker in the presence of higher governance (Nauman et al., 2023). This research suggests that servant leaders, directly and indirectly, play a significant role in project success and improve followers' trust in the construction industry in Pakistan.

A second correlational predictive study by Mozammel and Abdulla (2024) investigated the impact of servant leadership HR managers on project success in the construction sector and whether interpersonal trust mediates this relationship along with the moderating roles of ethical work climate and project governance. The sample consisted of 336 construction project team members from the government and private sectors (Mozammel & Abdulla, 2024). Structural equation modeling was utilized to ascertain the results, which found that servant leadership has a direct positive effect on project success ($\beta = .313$, $p = 0.005$) (Mozammel & Abdulla, 2024). Additionally, interpersonal trust mediated the relationship ($\beta = .281$, $p = 0.001$), while ethical work climate ($\beta = .196$, $p = 0.001$) and project governance ($\beta = .447$, $p = 0.001$) moderate the relationship between servant leadership and interpersonal trust (Mozammel & Abdulla, 2024). This study highlights that when HR managers have servant leadership qualities, they directly affect project success. Moreover, interpersonal trust helps explain this positive impact, while further enhanced when those HR managers foster an ethical work climate and robust governance structures.

The third study by Hassan et al. (2021) is one of the most relevant to this research as it is a correlational predictive study exploring how servant leadership affects project success. Uncertainty was the moderator, while trust in leadership was the mediator in analyzing public and private sector construction companies from Rawalpindi and Islamabad, Pakistan (Hassan et al., 2021). Results gathered from 184 construction sector employees through several regression steps to determine that servant leadership has a positive effect on successful project outcomes ($\beta = 0.298$, $\Delta R = 0.168$) and trust in leadership ($\beta = 0.490$, $\Delta R = 0.240$). Moreover, trust in leadership impacts the success of project outcomes ($\beta = 0.298$, $\Delta R = 0.168$) and has also been found to mediate servant leadership and project outcomes ($\beta = 0.382$, $\Delta R = 0.146$) (Hassan et al., 2021). Additionally, Hassan et al. (2021) note that uncertainty moderates the relationship between servant leadership and trust in leaders, meaning that when servant leadership is high, uncertainty is low, increasing trust, and has the opposite effect when servant leadership is low in construction companies in Pakistan.

The final study by Jan (2025) is another correlational predictive study that is also relevant to the current research as it examines how servant leadership affects project success in the construction and telecommunication industries in Rawalpindi and Islamabad, Peshawar, Bannu and Karak, Pakistan. Trust in leadership was the mediating variable while project governance was the moderating variable (Jan, 2025). A total of 250 construction and telecommunication employee surveys were collected. SPSS and Amoos were used for analysis to determine that servant leadership has a significant positive effect on project success ($\beta = .681$, $p < .001$) (Jan, 2025). Additionally, it was found that trust in leadership partially mediates ($\beta = .442$, $p < .001$) the relationship between servant leadership and project success (Jan, 2025). Moreover, Jan (2025) found that project governance negatively moderates the relationship between servant leadership and project success ($\beta = 0.20$, $p < 0.01$). These findings by Jan (2025) suggest that servant leaders that promote trust amongst their followers can improve the success of projects in the construction and telecommunications sector in Pakistan, and can be enhanced by having less project governance.

These studies highlight the current book on the interconnections between these variables and emphasize the existing gaps. Hassan et al. (2021), Jan (2025), Mozammel and Abdulla (2024), and Nauman et al. (2023) explored how servant leadership influences project success, gathering data from construction project employees in Pakistan. These studies display a direct positive relationship between servant leadership and project success through interpersonal trust (Mozammel & Abdulla, 2024; Nauman et al., 2023) and trust in leaders (Hassan et al., 2021; Jan 2025) moderated by project governance, ethical work climate, uncertainty (Hassan et al., 2021; Mozammel & Abdulla, 2024; Nauman et al., 2023), while negatively moderated by project governance (Jan, 2025). These findings suggest that servant leadership is essential for managing construction projects in Pakistan (S. Ali et al., 2023; Hassan et al., 2021; Jan, 2025; Nauman et al., 2023) and Bahrain (Mozammel & Abdulla, 2024). Servant leadership is, directly and indirectly, effective when dealing with uncertainty and inconsistent levels of project governance (Hassan et al., 2021; Jan, 2025; Mozammel & Abdulla, 2024;
Nauman et al., 2023).

The book review highlights gaps in research, particularly the need for studies examining the relationship between servant leadership, trust in leaders, and IT project success in the United States. This study aimed to fill these gaps by focusing on how trust in leaders mediates the relationship between servant leadership and IT project success in technology project teams in the United States (Nauman et al., 2023). By addressing these gaps, this study enhances the understanding of leadership dynamics in IT project management and offers practical implications for improving project outcomes.

Problem Statement

It is not known if, or to what extent, trust in leaders mediates the relationship between servant leadership and IT project success dimensions of project management success, perception success, and result success within technology project teams. This study explores the relationship between servant leadership and project success by examining the role of mediating factors, such as trust in leaders. By gaining insights into project success factors at both the team and humanistic levels, the gap can be bridged between effective servant leadership and technology project teams, helping to improve the success of IT projects.

The population of interest includes individuals who are part of a technology project team within an IT project team in the United States and are 18 years or older. The population of interest is defined as anyone who could be impacted by the research (Casteel & Bridier, 2021). In comparison, the target population is a group of potential participants who are accessible and willing to participate (Casteel & Bridier, 2021). The target population for this research encompasses various roles within technology project teams:

portfolio managers, program managers, project managers, project coordinators, engineers, business analysts, scrum masters, delivery leads, delivery managers, product owners, product managers, designers, architects, developers, quality team members. The target population for this research encompasses various roles within technology project teams: portfolio managers, program managers, project managers, project coordinators, technology engineers, business analysts, scrum masters, delivery managers, product owners, and product managers, designers, architects, developers, quality team members. Additionally, this population includes part-time, fulltime, and seasonal employees and contractors in IT project teams. The data collection process will examine servant leadership's total and direct effects on IT project success and the indirect effects of trust in leaders on this relationship.

The high failure rate of technology projects is one of the most pressing issues in business today. According to the Standish Group International (2019), 83.9% of project fail globally, either partially or entirely, with 52% failing to deliver short-term project success benefits of scope, budget, or schedule. The IT project failure rate in the United States has risen to more than 60% after the COVID-19 pandemic due to extensive delays and stoppages (L. Ali et al., 2023). The global cost of failed technology projects is in the billions, underscoring the urgent need to develop leadership and team skills to improve project success (Schmidt, 2022). Therefore, understanding project success factors and failure is critical and a matter of immediate concern (Schmidt, 2022). By enhancing servant leadership training, these high failure rates and significant financial losses could be mitigated, along with improved project management practices within the IT sector. This study addresses practical and theoretical ways to improve the success of IT projects with followers' trust in their servant leaders. Hence, this study examined the extent to which trust in leaders mediates the relationship between servant leadership and IT project success by understanding the adult perceptions of IT project team members in the United States.

Summary

The book review section has explored the relationship between the servant leadership theory (Liden et al., 2015), the trust in leaders (TIL) model (Podsakoff et al., 1990), and the IT project success model (Harwardt, 2018). For this study, the servant leadership theory and model by Liden et al. (2015) is a univariate measure that identifies altruistic servant behaviors (Haq et al., 2022) in business environments. The TIL model by Podsakoff et al. (1990) evaluates the indirect relationship between followers' perceived trust in their leaders. This model helps to understand how trust mediates the impact of servant leadership on IT project outcomes. The IT project success model (Harwardt, 2018) examines the success of IT projects through the benefit evaluation dimensions of project management success, perception success, and result success. This study integrates theory and models to address the research questions and problem statement in a way that provides valuable insights into both the practical and theoretical aspects of the American information technologies industry. The findings could be necessary for each field, specifically the IT project sector. The 83.9% global IT project failure rate (Standish Group International, 2019) and a more than 60% post-COVID19 failure rate in the United States cost businesses billions annually, causing immediate concern (Schmidt, 2022).

During the investigation into the current book, several gaps have emerged regarding the effects of servant leadership on project success. The first three gaps involve a theoretical gap (Ellahi et al., 2022; Jan, 2025), a contextual gap (Nauman et al., 2022a), and a practical knowledge gap (Nauman et al., 2022b). These three gaps are to explore the human side of project management (Nauman et al., 2022b), enhance project team performance through trust in leaders (Nauman et al., 2022a), and use additional mediating variables closely related when integrated and solved using the mediating variable of trust in leaders. Recent studies have shown that servant leadership has a significant impact on project success (Ellahi et al., 2022; Jan, 2025; Malik et al., 2022; Nauman et al., 2022a; Nauman et al., 2022b) through team dynamics, such as team performance, effectiveness (Bilal et al., 2021; Ren et al., 2021; Ruiz-Palomino et al., 2023), team motivation (Ellahi et al., 2022), team goal clarity, team process clarity (Bilal et al., 2021), team cohesion (Khalil et al., 2025), emotional intelligence (Malik et al., 2022), knowledge sharing, collaborative culture (Nauman et al., 2022a), work engagement, project work withdrawal (Nauman et al., 2022b) and trust in leaders (Hassan et al., 2021; Jan, 2025). Although the exploration of the recommended mediating variable of the trust of leadership (Jan, 2025; Nauman et al., 2022a) was conducted in construction companies located in Pakistan, the relationship between servant leadership and project success has not been investigated within the IT industry (Nauman et al., 2023), or in the United States. This investigation uses trust in leaders as a mediating variable to investigate the human side of project management, addressing all three gaps simultaneously.

This study examines several additional gaps expressly and implicitly stated in that book, such as the population gap (Ellahi et al., 2022; Jan, 2025) and the industry gap (Nauman et al., 2023). The population gap is visible as the current book has conducted studies in Pakistan (Bilal et al., 2021; Ellahi et al., 2022; Jan, 2025; Nauman et al., 2022a; Nauman et al., 2022b), Afghanistan (Mombeuil et al., 2023), The Gaza Strip (Amuna et al., 2021), Indonesia (Little & Martens, 2024), Bahrain (Mozammel & Abdulla, 2024), and German-speaking European countries (Harwardt, 2018, 2020), and one limited NGO study within the United States (Mombeuil et al., 2023). At the same time, the industry gap exists because the current research revolves around NGOs (Ahmadzai, 2024; Amuna et al., 2021; Little & Martens, 2024; Malik et al., 2022; Mombeuil et al., 2023), construction (S. Ali et al., 2023; Hassan et al., 2021; Jan 2025; Mozammel & Abdulla, 2024; Nauman et al., 2023), software development (Ellahi et al., 2022).

Therefore, when integrating these six gaps and the studies by Hassan et al. (2021) and Jan (2025) help to develop the problem statement. It is not known if, or to what extent, trust in leaders mediates the relationship between servant leadership and IT project success dimensions of project management success, perceptions success, and result success within technology project teams. This further aligns with the purpose statement that includes the United States as the population of interest.

The book review explored the relationship between servant leadership theory (Liden et al., 2015), the trust in leaders model (Podsakoff et al., 1990), and the IT project success model (Harwardt, 2018). The study aims to address the high IT project failure rates by investigating how trust in leaders mediates the impact of servant leadership on IT project outcomes. Several gaps were identified, including theoretical, contextual, practical knowledge, population, and industry gaps. This study will focus on the IT industry in the United States, addressing these gaps by examining the human side of project management through the mediating variable of trust in leaders. Chapter 3, which follows, will detail the research methodology, including the study's purpose, research questions, hypotheses, and variables. It will discuss the rationale for the chosen methodology and design, review the population and estimated sample size, and outline the strategy for obtaining it. Finally, Chapter 3 will cover data collection, analysis procedures, and the assumptions and delimitations of the study.

Chapter 3: Methodology

Introduction

The purpose of this quantitative correlational predictive study was to examine if, and to what extent, trust in leaders mediates the relationship between servant leadership and IT project success dimensions of project management success, perception success, and result success within technology project teams in the United States. This problem was identified as a significant gap within the IT project management field, as discussed in Chapter 2. This research analytically examines three theoretical models and their instruments. These models were used to assess if trust in leaders explains the predictive correlation between servant leadership within the context of IT project dimensional aspects in the United States.

The book review was presented in Chapter 2, which examined the relationship between servant leadership (Liden et al., 2015), trust in leaders (Podsakoff et al., 1990), and project success models (Harwardt, 2018), along with current research surrounding these variables and their interconnections. The book review also revealed that high IT project failure rates in the United States could be mitigated by examining the mediating role of trust in leaders in the relationship between servant leadership and IT project outcomes. Several gaps were identified, including theoretical (Malik et al., 2022), contextual (Nauman et al., 2022a), practical knowledge (Nauman et al., 2022b), population (Ellahi et al., 2022; Jan, 2025), and industry gaps

(Nauman et al., 2023). Additionally, Hassan et al. (2021) and Jan (2025) examined a similar study to this research regarding servant leadership's impact on project success through trust in leaders, with the difference being within the construction sector in Pakistan. This highlights the significant gap within the heart of the problem space. Therefore, this study focuses on the IT industry in the United States, addressing these gaps by investigating the human side of project management through the mediating variable of trust in leaders.

This chapter outlines the methodology and design of the study, beginning with a discussion of its purpose. It then provides a detailed overview of the research approach, including the population descriptions, sample selection, instrumentation, data collection, and data analysis. The validity and reliability of the instruments, as established in previous research, will also be discussed. The chapter concludes with a discussion of the assumptions and delimitations of the study, which set the scope and boundaries of the research (Theofanidis & Fountouki, 2018). While necessary to maintain the manageability of the study, these delimitations may negatively influence the generalizability, validity, and applicability of the findings.

Chapter 2 explained the rationale for the research. Chapter 3 describes how the research will be conducted and how the research questions and hypotheses will be answered. At the end of this chapter, there will be a clear understanding of the study's alignment and procedures, from the choice of methodology and design to the analytic and ethical boundaries that assist in defining the purpose of this study.

Purpose of the Study

The purpose of this quantitative correlational predictive study was to examine if, or to what extent, trust in leaders mediates the relationship between servant leadership and IT project success dimensions of project management success, perception success, and result success within technology project teams in the United States. This study will use quantitative analysis to assess three research questions, each with a corresponding set of null and alternative hypotheses, within a correlational predictive study design. These questions and hypotheses consist of one predictor, one mediator, and three criterion variables. The following paragraphs briefly overview the data collection and analysis processes.

The first step in beginning the research is distributing the survey link developed using the Qualtrics© professional survey platform. Eighty-nine participants will be recruited using two sampling methods: convenience sampling using the Project Management Institute (PMI) and IT project management professional social media groups. Accepted participants will be asked to provide demographic information and complete a twenty-question survey combining servant leadership, three IT project success subscales, and trust in leaders. After collecting the required data, the OLS regression using the PROCESS macro v4.3, model 4 for SPSS (Hayes, 2018), will be used for analysis. This analysis will provide tabulated outputs containing the results of the indirect effects of trust in leaders on the relationship between servant leadership and the dimensions of IT project success. Lastly, the null hypobook for each research question will be rejected or retained depending on the outputs provided by SPSS. The remaining sections will further detail each of these critical steps. The hypotheses, variables, and research questions will be discussed next.

Research Questions and Hypotheses

The problem statement for this study is that it is not known if, or to what extent, trust in leaders mediates the relationship between servant leadership and IT project success dimensions of project management success, perception success, and result success within technology project teams. The data were collected using three instruments for servant leadership, trust in leaders, and IT project success. The following research questions and subsequent hypotheses drive the variables and data for this study:

RQ1: Does trust in leaders mediate the relationship between servant leadership and project management success?

$H1_0$: Trust in leaders does not significantly mediate the relationship between servant leadership and project management success.

$H1_a$: Trust in leaders does significantly mediate the relationship between servant leadership and project management success.

RQ2: Does trust in leaders mediate the relationship between servant leadership and perception success?

$H2_0$: Trust in leaders does not significantly mediate the relationship between servant leadership and perception success.

$H2_a$: Trust in leaders does significantly mediate the relationship between servant leadership and perception success.

RQ3: Does trust in leaders mediate the relationship between servant leadership and result success?

$H3_0$: Trust in leaders does not significantly mediate the relationship between servant leadership and result success.

$H3_a$: Trust in leaders does significantly mediate the relationship between servant leadership and result success.

Variables

This study focused on servant leadership as the predictor, trust in leaders as the mediator, and IT project success dimensions as the criterion variables. See Figure 1 for a visual representation of these variables; a further breakdown of this visual model can be explored in Figure 3 later in Chapter 3. Furthermore, the summary of the study variables is in Table 2 below.

Figure 1

Visual Mapping of Research Questions, Hypotheses, and Variables

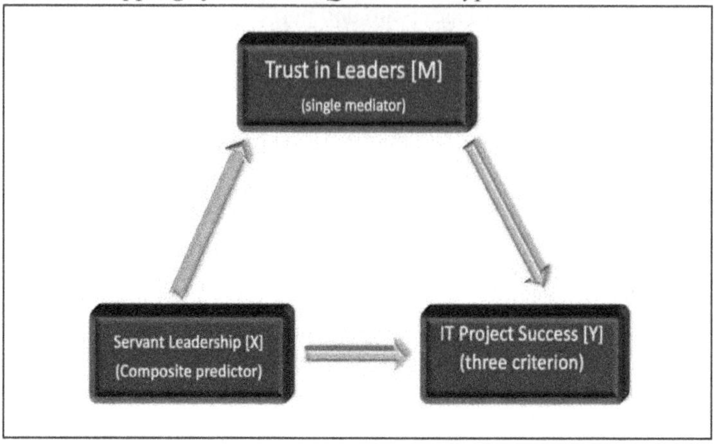

The predictor variable is servant leadership, conceptually defined as a leadership style that prioritizes the well-being of subordinates over the leader's interests (Ehrhart, 2004; Liden et al., 2015). Operationally, the SL variable is defined by a composite score from seven 7-stage Likert scale items, treated as ordinal data approximated to interval data (Norman, 2010), serving as a global measurement for SL as a predictor. This scale was created to provide a global composite variable for servant leadership, making servant leadership research more efficient (Liden et al., 2015). It provides a concise method to operationalize servant leadership, and the seven domains identified by Liden et al. (2008), initially using a 28-item scale. This SL-7 model allows for a global assessment of servant leadership and more efficient comparisons in various business settings and contexts (Liden et al., 2015). Furthermore, this model has been used in many current studies regarding team performance (Nauman et al., 2022a) and organizational citizenship behavior

(Özkan et al., 2023), which are significant aspects of project dynamics.

The mediator variable is trust in leaders (TIL), conceptually defined as the faith and devotion of subordinates to their leader (Podsakoff et al., 1990). Operationally, the TIL variable is defined by a composite score from six 7stage Likert scale items, treated as ordinal data approximated to interval data (Norman, 2010), which serves as the overall measurement for TIL. This scale was created to allow for a single composite score using two dimensions that comprise the trust in leaders variable. The model uses two dimensions, scored with three questions for follower faith and three questions for follower loyalty, combined to ascertain leaders' trust within IT project settings for this study. The TIL model by Podsakoff et al. (1990) was chosen as it has been used extensively as a mediating variable, such as ethical leadership impacts on project success
(Bhatti et al., 2021) and the effects of inclusive leadership on project citizenship behavior (Raiz et al., 2023). Therefore, the TIL model is the most appropriate mediating variable of trust in leaders for this study.

The IT project success model (ITPS) has three subscales, which will be individually measured using three simple linear regressions within the SPSS v29 with Hayes (2018) PROCESS macro v4.3 analysis. The overall conceptual definition for IT project success is a set of principles that evaluate the success of a project in terms of scope, budget, schedule, client and stakeholder perspective, along with financial and strategic objectives for the business from the management's perspective (Harwardt, 2018, 2020).

However, no composite score of IT project success will be analyzed for this study, only its three subdimensions. Operationally, IT project success is broadly defined as an aggregate of the dimensions of project management success (PM), perception success (PS), and result success (RS).

Project management success (PM), or short-term view, is conceptually defined as encompassing all items related to the planning and execution of an IT project and ensuring the achievement of project objectives regarding schedule, budget, scope, and resources (Harwardt, 2020). PM is operationally defined as a summarized IT project success subscale score. PM assesses success based on traditional project success factors, like the iron triangle of quality, schedule, and budget (Harwardt, 2020). Perception success (PS), the medium-term view, is defined by the different perspectives of the team members, clients, and end users on the success of IT projects (Harwardt, 2018). Operationally, PS is defined by the sum score on the IT project success subscale, measuring project success from both external and internal perspectives (Harwardt, 2018, 2020). The long-term view, result success (RS), is conceptually defined as estimating project success based on the financial or strategic benefits to the organization (Harwardt, 2020). Operationally, RS is defined by the sum score on the IT project success subscale, measuring success based on financial aspects, including the project's value and its impact on the organization (Harwardt, 2018).

Table 2

Summary of Study Variables

Variable	Conceptual Definition	Operational Definition	Measurement Level	Instrument/Data Source	SPSS Variable Name
Servant Leadership (Predictor)	A philosophical leadership style that looks for the well-being of subordinates ahead of their own (Liden et al., 2008, 2015)	Composite Score, 7 self-reported questions on servant leadership.	Ordinal approximated to interval (7-stage Likert scale)	Survey: Servant Leadership Scale (SL-7) (Liden et al., 2008, 2015).	SL
Trust in Leaders (Mediator)	The faith and devotion of subordinates to their leader (Podsakoff et al., 1990)	Composite Score, 6 self-reported questions on trust in leaders	Ordinal approximated to interval (7-stage Likert scale)	Survey: Trust in Leader Scale (TIL) (Podsakoff et al., 1990)	TIL
Perception Success (Criterion)	The success of an IT project (mid-term) that is based on the perceptions of the end user, client, or stakeholder perspectives (Harwardt, 2018).	IT project success 1st subscale: 3 selfreported questions focused on perception success.	Ordinal approximated to interval (5-stage Likert scale)	Questionnaire on IT Project Success (Harwardt, 2018).	PS
Result Success (Criterion)	The success of an IT project (long-term) is estimated based on the financial or strategic benefits to the firm (Harwardt, 2018).	IT project success 2nd subscale: 2 self-reported questions focused on result success.	Ordinal approximated to interval (5-stage Likert scale)	Questionnaire on IT Project Success (Harwardt, 2018).	RS

Project Management Success (Criterion)	The success of an IT project (short-term), from planning and execution to closure, ensures adherence to time, budget, scope, and resources (Harwardt, 2018).	IT project success approximated 3rd subscale: 2 questions focused on project management success.	Ordinal to interval self-reported (5-stage Likert scale)	Questionnaire on IT Project Success (Harwardt, 2018).	PM

The three dimensions of IT project success are viewed on a continuum in Figure 2 below. The ITPS model by Harwardt (2018) is the most suitable for this study as it considers the perspective of IT project leaders. Additionally, it has been used in studies regarding multiple IT project success dimensions (Harwardt, 2018). It has been used to determine the correlational predictive relationship between servant leadership behaviors and their impacts on the three dimensions (Harwardt, 2020). Therefore, since the ITPS by Harwardt (2018) frames this study and serves as the basis for conducting a mediation analysis, it was the most appropriate model for this study.

Figure 2

Chronological Valuation of the Success Dimensions

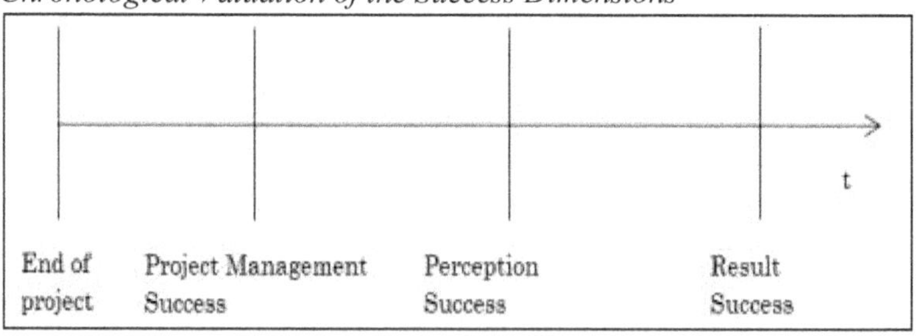

*Note.*Based onHarward(2018)

Rationale for a Quantitative Methodology

The purpose of this quantitative research was to ascertain if, and to what extent, trust in leaders mediates the relationship between servant leadership and project success within technology project teams. Using a quantitative approach depended on the philosophy, theoretical framework, research strategy, and factors related to the research problem that was examined (Mwansa et al., 2022). The relative strengths of the quantitative methodology include, but are not limited to, the ability to measure variables, objectively measure outcomes for future replicability, and generalize findings to larger populations. These strengths align with the problem statement goals, making it the most appropriate methodological approach for this study. The following paragraph discusses several additional empirically based characteristics of quantitative methodological research. These relative quantitative strengths are then shown, along with how they aligned with the goals of the research questions.

Researchers use the quantitative methodology to test hypotheses and explore the relationships between variables through statistical analysis (McDermott, 2023). Another characteristic of quantitative research was that it uses positivism as its philosophical framework (Ahmadin, 2022), which values objectivity (Abuhamda et al., 2021). Quantitative methodological research tests theories (Saha, 2022) using variables structured into research questions (Abuhamda et al., 2021), allowing researchers to examine their relationships through statistical evaluations (Hamida Bibi et al., 2022) of the null and alternative hypotheses using independent and dependent variables (McDermott, 2023). Additionally, the quantitative approach uses valid and reliable instruments (Abuhamda et al., 2021) that drew precise results (Ahmadin, 2022) from groups (Song, 2023) to generalize to the larger population (Hamida Bibi et al., 2022). This means that a researcher establishes the research problem and then formulates structured hypotheses that are statistically analyzed using specific instruments to help generalize to the entire population.

Reviewing examples of similar studies that use this methodological strategy is imperative to justify further use of the quantitative approach for this study. Harwardt (2020) conducted the most relevant study regarding this research, using the quantitative approach to examine the impacts of servant leadership behaviors on the dimensions of IT project success in IT project teams. Additionally, Nauman et al. (2023) utilized the quantitative methodology to examine whether trust mediated the impacts of servant leadership on project success in the construction industry. Therefore, after reviewing the attributes, aims of the study, and extant book in the field, the quantitative methodological approach was the most appropriate for this study. However, it was also essential to review which attributes of a qualitative approach were unsuitable in further justifying this research topic.

Obtaining a better understanding of the qualitative approach was essential to providing further justification for using the quantitative strategy. The qualitative methodology explores comprehensive, in-depth subjective experiences, meanings, and interpretations of word-formed data through open-ended interviews, observations, and focus groups (Busetto et al., 2020) regarding a phenomenon (Islam & Aldaihani, 2022) using subjective emotional interpretations (Afubwa & Kauka, 2023). Additionally, the qualitative approach promotes greater flexibility in the research questions, the type and quantity of data analyzed, and the selection of theoretical frameworks to effectively answer the research questions (Kiger & Varpio, 2020; Kim et al., 2017). This flexibility and data collection approach of the qualitative method do not align with the aims of the problem statement for this study, which is to statistically analyze a predictive relationship between variables to generalize to the larger population.

In conclusion, selecting an appropriate research strategy requires alignment with the specific methodology, the problem statement, and the research questions. The problem statement was aligned with the research questions, and both reflected that it was unknown to what extent trust in leaders mediated the relationship between servant leadership and the IT project success dimensions within technology project teams. The methodology and design choice are based on the crafted problem statement and the goals of the study (Asenahabi, 2019). Moreover, the strengths of the quantitative approach include measuring relationships objectively (Abuhamda et al., 2021) through statistically analyzing hypotheses and related variables (McDermott, 2023) using valid and reliable instruments (Abuhamda et al., 2021) to infer larger populations (Hamida Bibi et al.,

2022). In contrast, a qualitative strategy aims to obtain subjective (Afubwa & Kauka, 2023), in-depth information (Busetto et al., 2020) gathered on social phenomena (Islam & Aldaihani, 2022), allowing for more flexible designs (Kiger & Varpio, 2020; Kim et al., 2017). Therefore, the quantitative methodology was the most appropriately aligned approach to the problem statement, hypotheses, and related variables for this study.

Rationale for Research Design

This study employed a correlational predictive research design to ascertain to what extent trust in leaders mediated the relationship between servant leadership and IT project success among adult (18+) technology project team members in the United States. The correlational predictive design is instrumental in determining the predictive capacity of variables to predict the constructs (Cardoso-Pulido et al., 2022) of servant leadership's influence on IT project success factors, potentially explained through trust in leaders. Seeram (2019) posited that the correlational predictive design scrutinizes the predictability of relationships between predictor and criterion variables within theoretical frameworks. Correlational predictive studies can explain the extent of variance in the predictability of the criterion variable (Jenaro et al., 2020). While this study design does not establish a cause-andeffect relationship (Bloomfield & Fisher, 2019), it determines the magnitude and direction of the relationship between the variables (Taherdoost, 2022). To further substantiate the selection of the correlational predictive design, it is crucial to discuss why it was the most appropriate to answer the research questions for this study.

The research questions posed in this study aimed to ascertain the degree of mediation in the predictive relationship between servant leadership and IT project success dimension criteria. This study examined the extent of variable relationships, predictive capacity, and the extent of variance. However, this study design did not establish a causeand-effect relationship (Bloomfield & Fisher, 2019). Moreover, this study explored the presence of a mediating variable, trust in leaders, using primary data and self-reporting surveys (Radhakrishnan, 2013). Testing of a mediating variable inferred that a predictive relationship existed (Hayes, 2018) between servant leadership and IT project success, which was previously found in a similarly structured correlational predictive study (Harwardt, 2020). Therefore, the correlational predictive design was the most suitable approach for this research. However, examining other quantitative methodological designs is crucial to ensure the appropriateness of the correlational predictive design to answer the research questions for this research.

Alternative quantitative research designs include the experimental class, such as true-, pre-, and quasi-experimental—and the non-experimental class, including correlational or associative, comparative, and ex-post facto designs. True experimental designs are recognized as the highest standard in experimental research due to greater internal validity using a randomized control group (Novosel, 2022). Additionally, true experimental designs manipulate the independent variable to examine the impacts on the dependent variable and aim to establish a cause-and-effect relationship (Hunziker et al., 2021). In contrast, the pre-experimental study design involves the researcher selecting and assigning participants into groups without randomization (Białowąs et al., 2021). This design has limited internal and external validity due to the lack of a randomly selected control group (Apuke, 2017; Murta et al., 2021), making it less valid than the true experimental design. Quasiexperimental designs involve testing an intervention on nonrandomized groups (Duckett, 2021) or using nonrandomized independent variables (Taherdoost, 2022). As Novosel (2022) suggested, this design has less strength and control (Bloomfield & Fisher, 2019) than the true experimental design. However, the final design selection is based on the aim of the research questions.

Non-experimental designs, such as correlational or associative research designs, purposefully explore the associations between variables in the same population without utilizing prediction (Apuke, 2017). This design tests the existence of statistical associations between variables without drawing causal inferences (Dimarucot, 2022). A comparative research design, on the other hand, examines the differences in one or more variables between two or more groups (Radhakrishnan, 2013). The comparative design does not involve an intervention or manipulation of variables; instead, it compares two groups to obtain better evidence to suggest causal relationships (Apuke, 2017). Ex-post facto designs differ from comparative designs in that they utilize secondary data collection. According to Ahmadin (2022), the ex post facto design focuses on events that have already transpired. Radhakrishnan (2013) also noted that the ex post facto cannot determine causality.

Therefore, the correlational predictive design was the most suitable approach for this research, as it effectively examines the extent of variable relationships, predictive capacity, and the extent of variance between servant leadership and IT project success, mediated by trust in leaders (CardosoPulido et al., 2022; Seeram, 2019). This design was particularly appropriate for addressing the research questions, which aim to ascertain whether mediation exists in the predictive relationship between the variables (Hayes,

2018).

Population and Sample Selection

This study was conducted in the United States, and this section explains the population of interest, the target population, and the study sample. The general population, or population of interest, is characterized as individuals possessing the attributes of interest pertinent to the research (Andrade, 2021). For the general population, According to Zippia.com (2023), there are over 426,229 project managers in the United States, which represents only a fraction of total project teams, as each team typically consists of 6–10 members (Elad, 2023), bringing the general population to over 2.5 million. The population of interest for this study was all adult (18+) technology project team members in the United States. The target population is defined as the participants representing the study criteria the sampling frame was built around (Casteel & Bridier, 2021). The target population for this study was approximately 305,000 individuals and encompassed all adult (18+) technology project team members within the Project Management Institute (PMI) (Plan A) or IT project management social media groups (Plan B). This sample was a subset of the target population that could be generalized to the larger population (Casteel & Bridier, 2021). The inclusion criteria for this study included adults (18+) who were or had been members of technology project teams within the last three years and resided in the United States. Furthermore, they agreed to participate in and answer demographic and survey questions.

Estimated Sample Size

The planning phase of this study employed GPower, a priori power analysis tool designed to calculate the minimum sample size required for the requisite sample size (Faul et al., 2009). The GPower a priori analysis (Appendix F) determined a minimum sample size of 68 using the F tests family for multiple linear regression. GPower selections included a fixed model, R^2 deviation from zero, a medium effect size (f^2) of .15, a power ($1 - \beta$) error probability of .80, an error probability α of .05, and two predictor variables: servant leadership and the mediating variable of trust in leaders. Moreover, 30% was added for attrition and potential missing data buffers to accommodate potential assumption violations, providing the final target sample size of 89 participants. Keser et al. (2022) noted that there were no parametric tests for this analysis type as the bootstrapping method repeatedly resamples that data, reducing bias when parametric assumptions are violated.

Sampling Strategy, Recruitment Plan, and Site Authorization

This study used convenience sampling, utilizing the members from the Project Management Institute (PMI). Convenience sampling was a nonprobability method that drew from groups known to the researcher, offering a low-cost convenience option (Obilor, 2023). Recruitment plan A consisted of IT project team leaders and members who were recruited through approved internal message boards and distributed via an internal email to PMI members (PMI membership, 2023), which included a target population of about 2,503 members. Typical response rates for this recruitment type ranged from 9% for organizational studies, 17% for strategic management studies, and up to 71–74% for management studies (Holtom et al., 2022). Therefore, a baseline range of

5%–10% of the target population was expected to be sufficient for this study.

To conduct research, PMI required GCU's IRB approval before granting site authorization, although PMI did grant conditional approval (Appendix B). First, the application was submitted to GCU, including the email communication from the site indicating this requirement (Appendix B). GCU's IRB then provided a "Conditional Approval Letter," which was given to PMI to obtain official site authorization. Once the site authorization was received from PMI, it was resubmitted to GCU's IRB for final approval.

Contingency plan B involved utilizing Project Management Groups via Facebook and LinkedIn professional group pages, using convenience sampling, meaning participants found the digital survey flyer posted on social media groups (Casteel & Bridier, 2021). Plan A and Plan B ran concurrently for a month. For Plan B, the private

PMO LinkedIn group provided authorization with more than 106,466 members.

Additionally, one Facebook group approved the posting of the flyer: the Project Management Group, with more than 191,500 members. Aggregated, these plans provided a target population of nearly 300,000. Site authorization from these social media groups was obtained (Appendix B). If both Plan A and Plan B fail to obtain the minimum participant requirements after four weeks, the tertiary Plan C will be initiated. Plan C involves using the paid service Qualtrics© to disseminate the survey. Plan C was employed as a final resort to maintain cost-effectiveness when the four-week data collection timeframe failed to meet the minimum requirements.

Instrumentation and Research Materials

This research employed three established instruments to gather primary data in response to the three research questions, which encompass one predictor variable (servant leadership), one mediator (trust in leaders), and three criterion variables (subscales for IT project success factors). The subsequent sections will detail the development, structure, item types, scoring, measurement scale, and empirical history for each instrument. A final subsection examines demographic and organizational information.

Permissions and appropriate licensure for all three instruments were obtained and documented (Appendix C). All instruments in this study used Likert scale responses, which, according to Norman (2010), generate ordinal data approximated to interval data for analysis.

Research Data

Servant Leadership Model (SL-7). The SL-7 is a single global measure of servant leadership and is noted in book as reviewed for validity and reliability. This study utilized the SL-7 short-form model developed initially, refined, and operationalized by Liden et al. (2008) with a 28-item instrument known as the SL-28. The SL-7 was developed by Liden et al. (2015) as a composite scored global model to help enhance the practicality and speed of servant leadership research. Moreover, Liden et al. (2015) developed the SL-7 to provide a shorter measure of servant leadership while maintaining the same levels of validity and reliability as the original scale. To achieve this, one item was selected from each of the seven core dimensions of servant leadership represented in the SL-28. The new scale was tested across three studies, utilizing Cronbach's alpha to determine internal consistency. Additionally, factor loading was used to evaluate convergent validity, while criterion-related validity was tested using concurrent validity correlations with the SL-28 and hierarchical linear modeling. These methods confirmed the accuracy and strong correlation of the SL-7 with the original SL-28 scale. The SL-28 and the SL-7 models are the only two that Liden et al. (2008, 2015) have developed and used in current servant leadership book.

The short version, or the SL-7 model, was utilized for this study.

The SL-7 scale is used to measure seven dimensions of servant leadership: emotional healing, creating value for the community, conceptual skills, empowerment, helping subordinates grow and succeed, putting subordinates first, and behaving ethically. The SL-7 uses a seven-question, 7-item Likert scale, with responses ranging from 1 (strongly disagree) to 7 (strongly agree). The items included in this instrument,
(Appendix E), include "My leader can tell if something work-related is going wrong.", "My leader makes my career development a priority.", "I would seek help from my leader if I had a personal problem.", " My leader emphasizes the importance of giving back to the community.", "My leader puts my best interests ahead of his/her own.", "My leaders give me the freedom to handle difficult situations in the way that I feel is best.", and "My leader would NOT compromise ethical principles in order to achieve success." The predictor variable will be measured as ordinal approximated to interval. The instrument will be scored by summing up the values of the seven questions (for each participant) and dividing them by the number of questions to obtain the overall average.

The SL-7 has been used in various current studies focusing on the impacts of servant leadership on business employee-level outcomes. For example, Abiya and Martdianty (2022) found that servant leadership significantly affects employee innovative work behavior in a study involving 204 millennial workers across various industries in Indonesia. Swanson et al. (2022) also demonstrated that servant leadership positively impacts employee well-being, life satisfaction, teamwork, and physical health in a study with 489 North American sports industry participants.

Trust in Leader Scale (TIL). Podsakoff et al. (1990) developed the TIL to understand and measure the faith and loyalty of followers to their leaders within a singledimensional model. The TIL builds on earlier research that focused on loyalty to the leader (Giffin, 1967; Rotter, 1967) and interpersonal trust (Cook & Wall, 1980). Podsakoff et al. (1990) incorporated the dimension of faith in leaders, focusing on the followers' perspectives. Additionally, Podsakoff et al. (1990) introduced the second dimension, loyalty in leaders, and created the current operationalized TIL used in extant book. The TIL was developed by Podsakoff et al. (1990) through a thorough book review process, item generation, and an expert evaluation using the Qsort methodology. Confirmatory factor analysis (CFA) was also performed using the TuckerLewis Index (TLI) and the Comparative Fit Index (CFI) (Podsakoff et al., 1990). Cronbach's alpha was used to determine the internal consistency. Podsakoff et al. (1990) tested for discriminant and convergent validity using correlation analysis with other constructs, such as transformational leadership, general trust, Leader-Member Exchange (LMX), and Organizational Commitment scales.

The TIL scale consists of six questions measured using a seven-item Likert scale, with responses ranging from 1 (strongly disagree) to 7 (strongly agree), as developed by Podsakoff et al. (1990). The instrument items, (Appendix E), included are: "I feel quite confident that my leader will always try to treat me fairly.", "My manager would never try to gain an advantage by deceiving workers.", "I have complete faith in the integrity of my manager/supervisor.", "I feel a strong loyalty to my leader.", "I would support my leader in almost any emergency.", and one reverse-coded item of "I have a divided sense of loyalty toward my leader." This scale will measure the mediator variable, ordinal approximated to an interval. The instrument will be scored by summarizing the values of the six questions (for each participant) and dividing them by the number of questions to obtain the overall average.

The TIL has been used as a mediator in recent studies. For example, Bhatti et al. (2021) conducted a study with 175 project team members within software companies in Pakistan using the identical TIL model in this research. They found that leader trust mediates the relationship between ethical leadership and project success. Moreover, a study by Khawar et al. (2023) examined 130 management leaders within the private hospital sector in Pakistan and found that trust in leader mediated the relationship between servant leadership and job performance.

IT Project Success Model and Dimensions. This model was initially created through a qualitative study in which the first IT project success model was developed using the managers' perspective (Harwardt, 2016). Harwardt (2018) further developed and operationalized the ITPS model, which consists of three dimensions to assess the success of projects: result success, perception success, and project management success. These three dimensions of the ITPS model represent different project success benefits across short-, medium-, and long-term perspectives. The ITPS model was created to fill the gap in specific tools for assessing IT project success from a management viewpoint (Harwardt, 2018, 2020). An initial set of criteria was created in a qualitative study with project managers and executives by Harwardt (2016). That set of criteria was used in a quantitative study where a survey was administered to 646 participants and analyzed using structural equation modeling (SEM) (Harwardt, 2018). The study's outcome by Harwardt (2018) created the final model of IT project success with three dimensions that accurately reflect IT project success. Construct validity was tested using confirmatory factor analysis (CFA), discriminant validity was tested using the Fornell and Larcker (1981) criterion, convergent validity was tested using average extracted variance (AVE), content validity was tested using a comprehensive book review, expert review by industry experts (Harwardt, 2018), and qualitative research (Harwardt, 2016). Reliability was tested for internal consistency using Cronbach's alpha, indicator reliability analysis, and the SEM.

The three dimensions of the ITPS model were developed using the same testing but with insights from Harwardt (2016), who examined the criteria of ITPS and categorized the benefits over a continuum. These benefits were divided into three dimensions based on short-, medium-, and long-term IT project success time frames (Harwardt, 2018). The original model included 14 success criteria, and through SEM and a quantitative study

(Harwardt, 2018), the three dimensions were highly correlated with two subdimensions each, forming the final model that will be used in this study.

The ITPS is divided into three individual dimensions separated into a sevenquestion, 5-item Likert scale, with responses from 1 (strongly disagree) to 5 (strongly agree). As a note, there is no current aggregated scoring model for the three dimensions; therefore, these seven questions are divided into three items for project management success, two for perception success, and two for result success. Moreover, there will be no overall score for the ITPS model. Each dimension was assessed as an individual criterion variable, measured on an ordinal scale, and approximated to an interval scale. For example, each participant received three unique scores, one for each dimension, without an overall ITPS model score.

Project management success evaluates short-term success and includes the subdimensions of implementation and cooperation. This dimension encompasses the classic

Iron Triangle criteria of schedule, budget, quality, and communication (Harwardt, 2020). The three project management success dimensional items (Appendix E) are "The project planning is perceived as successful.", "The project management is highly efficient.", and "The project is conducted without serious incidents." Perception success assesses the medium-term success encompassing the external and internal perspectives, considering employees, end-users, customers, and stakeholder viewpoints (Harwardt, 2020). It consists of two items (Appendix E): "All stakeholders are satisfied with the project." and "The stakeholders have a positive perspective on the project." Lastly, result success represents the long-term view of IT project success, containing the sub-dimensions of project value and organizational impact, focusing on the financial and strategic aspects of IT project success (Harwardt, 2020). Result success consists of two items (Appendix E): "The project result is rated as successful.", and "The project result complies with the goals related to it."

Since the development of the model, only Harwardt (2020) conducted a single study within German-speaking countries, which also utilized 646 participants from the European Project Management Institute and other project management professionals, that found that servant leadership impacts IT project success and related dimensions that further provided validity and reliability of the model. While no other study has utilized the ITPS outside of Harwardt (2020), 44 articles have cited the study on the impacts of servant leadership behaviors and IT project success, indicating its growing recognition in IT industry book.

Additional Data

Demographic data was gathered in this research as it is crucial to acquire information from current project team members. This data provides a complete view of today's IT projects, presenting insights from the perspective of team members and their representative organizations. Moreover, collecting and analyzing this demographic data contributes to a more thorough understanding of the research findings and their relevance to these individual team members and firms (Harwardt, 2020). The additional data ensures a comprehensive and informed approach to interpreting the study results.

The first set of demographic questions focused on the participants' attributes. These variables include age, gender, educational qualifications, professional experience, and project experience. Obtaining these demographic details help to understand the participants within the sample as they produce descriptive statistics that assist in classifying, breaking down the sample, and making valuable inferences about the broader target population. The second level of demographic data concerned organizationallevel variables, such as the participant's current business sector, employment status (contractor or full-time employee), employer size, and current management level. This data is essential for generating descriptive statistics and understanding the context of the sample.

Validity

This study employed three validated instruments: the Servant Leadership Model

(SL-7), the Trust in Leader Scale (TIS), and the IT Project Success (ITPS) model and its three dimensions. Validity, as defined by Heale and Twycross (2015), is the extent to which an instrument measures what it is intended to measure. The following paragraphs provide specific validity statistics, their development, usage, and the necessary licensing information obtained for each instrument.

Servant Leadership Model (SL-7)

The SL-7 was validated by Liden et al. (2015) using three studies in a single article for their short-form instrument development. These validation results are related explicitly to the SL-7 utilized, and no items will be altered from the seminal version for this study. The first study participants by Liden et al. (2015) involved 598 undergraduates, 218 graduates, and 131 undergraduates, confirming construct validity with confirmatory factor analysis (CFA) (CFI = .97, SRMR = .03, RMSEA = .06, x^2 (14, N = 598) = 45.36, $p < .01$). Convergent validity was supported with Pearson's correlations ranging from .95 to .97 (Liden et al., 2015). Their second study sample used two distinct participant groups, consisting of 174 leader-follower dyads and 378 employees and managers, which were tested for construct validity using CFA between the SL-7: CFI = 1.00, RMSEA = .00, SRMR

[within] = .00, SRMR [between] = .04, AIC

= 2660.50, x^2 (2, N = 378) = .12; and the SL-28: CFI = 1.00, RMSEA = .00, SRMR [within] = .00, SRMR [between] = .04, AIC =2581.57, x^2 (2, N = 378) = .19, which further demonstrates criterion, concurrent, and predictive validities (Liden et al., 2015). Furthermore, Liden et al.'s (2015) third study used to develop the SL-7 involved 71 work teams, 304 employees, and 60 managers, confirmed criterion validity with CFA (CFI = .95, SRMR = .08, RMSEA = .09; x^2 (246) = 382.81, $p < .001$). Fornell and Larcker

(1981) were used for convergent validity, with an AVE of .63 (Liden et al., 2015). The content to be used is identical to the original; Elsevier owns the copyrights to Liden et al. (2015). Licensure approved, permitting the reuse of a book/book in print and electronic formats (Appendix E).

Trust in Leader Scale (TIL)

Developed by Podsakoff et al. (1990), the TIL was validated with 988 employees from a multinational petrochemical company. Construct validity was confirmed using the Tucker-Lewis Index for the single-dimensional model (TLI = .96; x^2 (9) = 105.63, $p <$ .001) (Podsakoff et al., 1990). Discriminant validity was supported by the Fornell and Larcker (1981) criterion, showing unique constructs (Podsakoff et al., 1990). The trust relationship full model overall goodness of fit indices (x^2 = 4878.0, *df* = 1241, TLI = .88) with chi-squared differences for the direct effects were calculated as (Δx^2 = 1292.4, *df* = 5, p = .04) (Podsakoff et al., 1990).

Moreover, the TIL was found to mediate the relationship between transformational leadership and follower citizenship behaviors, accounting for 85% of the variance, proving to be a valid mediating model measurement (Bhatti et al., 2021). Bhatti et al. (2021) further validated the TIL, confirming its fit through CFA (x^2 (269) = 499.873, $p < 0.001$, CFI = 0.951, IFI = .946, TLI = .951, RMSEA = 0.070) and demonstrating convergent and discriminant validity using AVE greater than .05. In conclusion, based on the tests for validity along with a similar study's mediating relationship, there appears to be a strong fit for this study. These validation findings relate to the seminal version of this instrument created by Podsakoff et al. (1990). This instrumentation will be utilized in its original form; no alterations to the instrument will be used. Elsevier owns the copyrights for Podsakoff et al. (1990), and licensure was approved, permitting reproduction in both electronic and print formats (Appendix E). The content for the trust-inleaders model was the same as the original, with no alterations.

IT Project Success Model and Subscales

The ITPS model, developed by Harwardt (2018), measures IT project success through project management, perception, and result success dimensions. Each of the dimensions of the ITPS was tested for individual content validity, providing evidence of goodness of fit for the overall model $x^2(410) = 1059.149$, df=410, $x^2/df = 2.583$, RMSEA

= .500, RMR = .045, SRMR = .037, TLI = .947, CFI = .953 (Harwardt, 2018).

Convergent validity was supported with AVE values above 0.5 for all dimensions (Fornell & Larcker, 1981), perception success (.739), project management success (.801), and result success (.751) (Harwardt, 2018). Discriminant validity was confirmed using structural equation modeling estimated standardized path coefficients for perception success ($R^2 = .678$, $p < .001$), project management success ($R^2 = .747$, $p < .001$), and result success ($R^2 = .695$, $p < .001$) (Harwardt, 2018).

Harwardt (2020) further validated the model with 568 project management professionals, confirming its robustness in a study examining servant leadership's impact and project success. These dimensions also represent different stages of the project success evaluation timeline. Therefore, this model fits this study well and will provide the necessary data to answer all research questions. Moreover, no other forms of this instrument have been created in the book, and this study will also use the original version of the ITPS as developed by Harwardt (2018). This instrument is distributed under the Creative Commons Attribution Noncommercial License (CC B 4.0), which permits the use, distribution, and reproduction with proper accreditation. The ITPS model used in this study was identical to the original by Harwardt (2018, 2020).

Reliability

Reliability Procedures

This research employs three tools: the SL-7, TIL, and ITPS models' subdimensions. The internal reliability of each tool will be assessed using Cronbach's alpha. If the results fall between .7 and .9, it indicates that the tools used in the study are internally consistent (Sürücü & Maslakçı, 2020). If the internal consistency score is less than .7, SPSS will be used to conduct a reliability analysis to identify which items in the scale contribute to this low value. The analysis should be done at the individual item level, and items closest to zero are removed (Churchill, 1979) and reassessed before running the data analysis. The historical and current reliability of each tool in the study will be detailed in the following subsections and Table 3 below.

Servant Leadership Model (SL-7)

The Servant Leadership (SL-7) scale, developed by Liden et al. (2015), is a concise, global, unidimensional model derived from the SL-28. It encapsulates seven aspects of servant leadership, focusing on leaders prioritizing their subordinates' welfare over their interests (Liden et al., 2008, 2015). The SL-7 scale's internal consistency ranges from .80 to .87 (Liden et al., 2015). Recent studies (Babalola et al., 2023; Jang et al., 2023; Swanson et al., 2022; Wang et al., 2022; Zada et al., 2022) have confirmed its reliability, with Cronbach's alpha values ranging from .74 to .95 (Table 3). Thus, this instrument was deemed reliable and directly relates to the version used in this study.

Trust in Leaders Scale (TIL)

The Trust in Leaders (TIL) model, developed by Podsakoff et al. (1990), is a unidimensional measure of followers' trust in their leaders. It uses a 6-item scale to measure follower faith and loyalty (Podsakoff et al., 1990). With Cronbach's alpha of .87, the TIL model exhibits high internal consistency (Podsakoff et al., 1990). It has been used in recent research (Baquero, 2023; Islam et al., 2024; Khawar et al., 2023; Rafiq et al., 2022; Raiz et al., 2023) and has proven reliable in various contexts and situations, with internal consistency levels ranging from .71 to .93 (Table 3). Therefore, this instrument was found to be reliable and fully relates to the instrumentation version used in this research.

IT Project Success Model Subscales

The ITPS and its subscales of perception success, project management success, and result success, are used to evaluate the success of an IT project from three benefit time frames. The Cronbach's alpha for each ITPS subdimension is .923 for project management success, .849 for perception success, and .847 for result success (Harwardt, 2018). These figures were obtained from a study involving IT project management team members in German-speaking countries. Harwardt (2020) conducted a subsequent study with a similar professional group, yielding Cronbach's alpha values of .921 for project management success, .865 for perception success, and .850 for result success. These results indicate a robust internal reliability for this model within the specific demographic of IT project management team members, making it a valuable tool for this research. The three ITPS dimensions of project management success, perception success, and result success are found to be reliable (Table 3). Additionally, these are the exact versions that were utilized in this study.

Table 3

Reliability of Instruments

Instrument	Questions	Cronbach Alpha or Range	ge from Current Research
SL-7: Servant leadership	7	.80 – .89	.74 – .95
TIL: Trust in Leaders	6	.87	.71 – .93
ITPS: Perception Success (PS)	2	.849	.865
ITPS: Project Management Success (PM)	3	.923	.921
ITPS: Result Success (RS)	2	.848	.850

Data Collection and Management

Data Collection Process

The first step in the data collection process was to obtain all necessary instrument permissions (Appendix E), as well as site authorizations (Appendix B). Prior to the recruitment of participants from any of the sampling plans, this research was subject to and approved by the academic quality review (AQR) and GCU Institutional Review Board (IRB). After these official approvals were obtained, recruitment began with sampling Plan A, while Plan B was concurrently running, discussed further in later paragraphs. This study has three sampling plans: Plan A involved the PMI, Plan B used professional social media groups, and Plan C used the paid services platform provided by Qualtrics©. For sampling Plan A, the Qualtrics© link was sent through the official PMI research request, which took approximately 72 hours to incorporate into their internal systems. The PMI (1) posted the survey flyer and Qualtrics© link on their internal discussion boards and (2) distribute the link through their internal email system, which excludes all members who have opted out of receiving emails from PMI. Sampling plan

A was used until (1) the sample size was reached or (2) 30 days have passed.

For sampling Plan B, survey flyers were posted on social media to invite participants to the study when the participants enter the flyer on the authorized social media site. The flyer provided the inclusion and exclusion criteria statements to allow participants to decide whether they meet the requirements for the study. To be included, participants must be adults (18+) and currently, or in the last three years, be IT project team members in the United States. They could not participate if they were under 18, have not been a project team member in the last three years, and or do not live in the United States. And if the participant meets the inclusion criteria, they could choose to proceed with the study. In that case the participant meets the inclusion criteria, they selected the Qualtrics© survey link within the flyer. This link directed them to the informed consent within the Qualtrics© survey platform. This ensured that each participant understand the purpose, participation risks, and benefits of partaking in this research. Respecting the well-being of participants is of the utmost importance and aligns with user principles and doctoral frameworks that can mitigate negative perceptions of data collection (Burkhardt et al., 2022). If the participant selected the "I agree" button on the informed consent page, they entered the demographics portion of the survey, followed by the instrument surveys. If participants selected the "I do not agree" button on the informed consent page, they were directed to the end of the survey page and thanked for their time. Additionally, in the case that sampling Plans A and B failed to reach the required sample size after 30 days, Plan C would be initiated and allow the Qualtrics© team to obtain the remaining sample size, as a last resort via the Qualtrics© paid survey service.

Regardless of the sampling plan, the Qualtrics© link sent the qualified participants to the informed consent page of the survey. If the informed consent was agreed to, participants were directed to the demographic phase of the survey, where they provided their age, gender, educational qualifications, professional experience (number of years), and project experience (number of years). In the following phase, participants provided their current business sector, employment status (contractor or full-time employee), the size of the business (number of employees), and their current management level (first-, middle-, and senior levels).

Once the demographic questions were completed, participants were directed to the 20-item self-reported research survey instruments administered in a single session via Qualtrics©. The survey timing, including demographic information and survey instrument, took no more than 10 minutes to complete. This single aggregated survey includes three instruments, which will be scored as follows:

1. The Servant Leadership (SL-7) scale consisted of seven questions scored on a 7point Likert scale. To calculate the overall servant leadership score, each participant's responses are summed up and then divided by the number of questions, providing an average score for each participant. A higher average score indicates that the leader displays greater servant leadership behaviors, while a lower average score indicates lower levels of these behaviors.

2. The Trust in Leader (TIL) scale, consisted of six questions, and were measured using a 7-point Likert scale. To calculate the overall trust score, the individual scores for each question will be summed up and then divided by the number of questions, providing an average score for each participant. A higher average score indicates greater faith and loyalty in their leader than a lower average score.

3. The IT project success (ITPS) model utilized three individual subscales of project management success. Each subscale was assessed

using a 5-point Likert scale. The project management success (PM) subscale included three questions, the perception success (PS) subscale had two questions, and the result success (RS) subscale had two questions. For each subscale, participant responses were summed up and then divided by the number of questions in that subscale, for example, three for project management success, to provide an average score. No aggregated scale was aggregated, as there was no overall ITPS score. Higher scores indicate greater perceived project success across three different benefit time frames, while lower scores indicate lower perceived project success levels for those time frames.

The survey remained open in Qualtrics© until the required sample size was reached. Data collected was then downloaded from the Qualtrics© website directly into SPSS v29, using the Qualtrics© SPSS export tool.

Management of this data will be addressed in the following sub-section.

Data Management Procedures

All data collected from the participants via the Qualtrics© survey will be stored in two locations. According to Hart et al. (2016), this protects against data loss and recommends keeping data in multiple locations. Only authorized personnel with proper authority and permission can access this data: the book chair, committee, and AQR reviewer, as the data will be in the LDP Folder. The data is stored securely using a password-protected external hard drive, locked in a fingerprint-secured safe in the researcher's home, preventing loss or theft (Scope et al., 2022). After three years, the hard drive will be deleted and then put through a factor reset and purge, rendering any possible data unrecoverable and unusable (Scope et al., 2022). No other forms of data collection, either digital or written, will be gathered. All GCU IRB guidelines were and will be followed during and after the book research process.

To maintain confidentiality and participant honesty, all participants conducted the survey anonymously. The Qualtrics© survey platform deidentifying selection was used, meaning that any potential information, such as internet protocol (IP) addresses, were not a part of the data collection process, removing any identifiable information within the data set prior to SPSS input. The data was analyzed using appropriate statistical software, SPSS v29, in the case of this study. The raw data was kept separate from the analysis to maintain data integrity. After the study is completed, the data will be retained for three years per GCU data storage policy (Administrators and the Responsible Conduct of Research, 2021). Once the retention period is over, the data will be deleted and written over from the external hard drive using a complete hard drive purge, returning it to factory settings.

Data Analysis Procedures

Data Cleaning and Preparation

After achieving the necessary sample size, data was transferred from Qualtrics© to a CSV file, then imported into Microsoft Excel for cleaning. Duplicate entries were identified and removed using Excel's VLOOKUP function. IP addresses were not collected in the dataset, as the Qualtrics© survey platform removes that data from being included in the data collection process. Any errors in data transfer were fixed appropriately when downloading the Qualtrics© data and migrating to Excel. Missing or incomplete surveys were excluded from the data. Outliers were handled on a case-bycase basis. Each scale was scored according to its technical documentation, and the cleaned data has been stored on an encrypted hard drive (Scope et al., 2022). The Excel file was then loaded into SPSS v29 for analysis. This Excel file was unaltered to ensure the availability of a recoverable dataset. Additionally, a copy of this file was saved in the LDP for committee and AQR review.

Descriptive Statistics

Constructs are established to facilitate the collection of descriptive and demographic data prior to the instrumentation phase of the survey. Demographic data for the study included gender, education level, work experience, industry sector, contractor status, organizational size, and management level. This demographic information contributes to a thorough understanding of the participants, their roles, experiences, and the sizes of the businesses they are employed in. The demographic descriptive statistics are divided into two categories: the dichotomous measures of gender and contractor status which analyzed the frequency distribution, percentages, and mode, while the ordinal measured responses analyzed the frequency distribution, percentages, median, and mode. These were conducted to understand the distribution and most common responses.

Descriptive statistics for the study variables analyzed distribution, normality, measures of central tendency, variability, and shape for categorical variables and additional descriptive mean, median, range, variance, standard deviation, z-skewness, and z-kurtosis for continuous variables. The descriptive statistics were analyzed for each variable using SPSS software. The results of these demographics and the study variables will be reported in Chapter 4.

Reliability of Instruments

Reliability is used to check the internal consistency of the instruments within a study. Internal consistency is measured using one of the most widely used methods, Cronbach's alpha (Amirrudin et al., 2023). This method is most effective when the instruments in the study have multiple items to analyze (Kimberlin & Winterstein, 2008).

According to Chan and Idris (2017), Cronbach's alpha is calculated as a range from zero to one, with levels greater than >.70 showing higher levels of reliability. The internal consistency for this study was calculated using Cronbach's alpha for each variable and each dimension of IT project success. Low correlation items, meaning less than < .70, were removed from the data as it would not be deemed reliable to conduct statistical analysis on those items.

Tests of Assumptions

The Hayes' (2018) PROCESS macro was used for mediation analysis, employing OLS regression (Abu-Bader & Jones, 2021; Clement & Bradley-Garcia, 2022).

Assumptions include:

1. Independence of Observations. The observations should be independent of each other. The SPSS v29 Durbin-Watson test can be run to ensure that autocorrelation or serial correlation does not exist in the data.

2. Test for Outliers. This test can be examined using the casewise diagnostics output table in SPSS v29. Outliers should be evaluated case-by-case to determine whether they are due to data entry errors, missing data, or genuine outliers (Vinisha & Sujihelen, 2022).

3. Linearity. This assumption can be explored through visual inspection of a scatterplot. A linear relationship, either positive or negative, must be present for the mediation analysis to be utilized and be relatively straight (Laerd Statistics, 2022).

4. Homoscedasticity. This assumption, also known as constancy of variance, can be visually checked in using a plot of studentized residuals versus unstandardized predicted values. (Laerd Statistics, 2022).

5. Normality of Residuals. This assumption requires that the residuals be normally distributed and can be assessed by examining a histogram or a normal P-P plot (Laerd Statistics, 2022).
6. Multicollinearity. This assumption requires that the predictor variables not have a correlational relationship or be highly correlated to each other (Laerd Statistics, 2022). It can be identified by carefully examining the variance inflation factor (VIF) (Kyriazos & Poga, 2023).

If assumptions are violated, no parametric test will be used. This is due to the robustness of bootstrapping used in the OLS regression analysis (Keser et al., 2022). However, if assumptions are violated, statistical process checks will be conducted to normalize the data before running the OLS regression analysis.

Data Analysis Statistical Procedures

It is not known if, or to what extent, trust in leaders mediates the relationship between servant leadership and IT project success dimensions of project management success, perception success, and result success within technology project teams. Three mediation analyses, using servant leadership as the predictor, trust in leaders as the mediator, and IT project success dimensions (project management success, results success, and perception success) as criterion variables. Here are the research questions and hypotheses for this study:

RQ1: Does trust in leaders mediate the relationship between servant leadership and project management success?

$H1_0$: Trust in leaders does not significantly mediate the relationship between servant leadership and project management success.

$H1_a$: Trust in leaders does significantly mediate the relationship between servant leadership and project management success.

RQ2: Does trust in leaders mediate the relationship between servant leadership and perception success?

$H2_0$: Trust in leaders does not significantly mediate the relationship between servant leadership and perception success.

$H2_a$: Trust in leaders does significantly mediate the relationship between servant leadership and perception success.

RQ3: Does trust in leaders mediate the relationship between servant leadership and result success?

$H3_0$: Trust in leaders does not significantly mediate the relationship between servant leadership and result success.

$H3_a$: Trust in leaders does significantly mediate the relationship between servant leadership and result success.

A simple mediation analysis will be used, as each research question consists of a predictor variable that impacts a criterion variable, as explained through a single mediating variable (Igartua & Hayes, 2021). The statistical analysis tool used in this study is Hayes' (2018) PROCESS macro v4.3 for SPSS. This tool explores the indirect effects of one or more mediating or moderating variables on the direct effect relationship between an explanatory and response variable (Clement & Bradley-Garcia, 2022). Hayes' (2018) PROCESS uses OLS regression that produces 5,000 bootstrap intervals that can overcome minor violations of homoscedasticity (Hayes, 2018) and normality assumptions (Keser et al., 2022) while minimizing Type 1 error rates (Abu-Bader & Jones, 2021) and the number of squared errors (Saryani, 2022). In summary, using the OLS regression method, the Hayes (2018) PROCESS macro is an appropriate tool for examining the mediating effects of trust in leaders on the relationship between servant leadership and IT project success factors.

The Hayes (2018) PROCESS macro was downloaded from the Hayes website and then extracted and installed into SPSS v29 for use in the analysis. The cleaned and prepared Microsoft Excel file was then uploaded into SPSS. In SPSS, 'Analyze' was selected in the drop-down menu, then 'Regression' was selected, and finally, 'PROCESS v4.3.' The PROCESS macro dialog box then appeared, and a model number needed to be chosen. Klompstra et al. (2022) state that model 4 of the PROCESS macro (Hayes, 2018) should be selected to calculate simple mediating effects (See Figure 3). For this study, the '(X) variable' is servant leadership, the '(Y_1) variable' is project management success, and the mediating 'Mediator (M)' is trust in leaders. Bootstraps were set to 5,000, with a 95% confidence interval. Further, selected PROCESS options included showing the total effect model and effect size for inclusion in the output. Once input into model 4 of the

PROCESS macro dialog box, ‘OK’ was be selected, and the analysis output was completed. The analysis outputs will be displayed and discussed further in Chapter 4.

Figure 3

Hayes (2018) PROCESS Mediation Model 4 Diagram for the Current Study

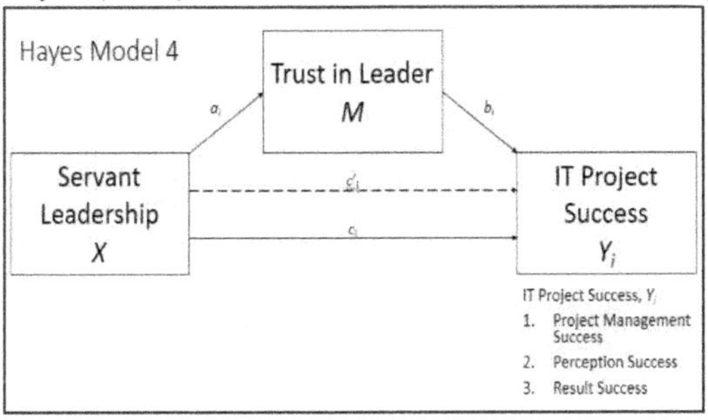

Next, the PROCESS macro creates an output table that reviewed the variables' direct and indirect effects. The first step in a mediation analysis is to evaluate the direct effect between servant leadership (X) and project management success (Y_1). The second is to examine the direct effect of servant leadership (X) on trust in leaders (M). The last is to review the indirect effect of servant leadership (X) on project management success (Y_1) through trust in leaders (M). Suppose the regression coefficients and the upper and lower bootstrap confidence intervals show that the indirect effect does not include zero

(Clement & Bradley-Garcia, 2022). In that case, there is an indication that trust in leaders (M) has a mediating effect on the relationship between servant leadership (X) and project management success (Y_1).

Furthermore, if the indirect effect (a_1*b_1) confidence intervals do not contain zero, it can be determined that mediation is present in the predictive relationship between servant leadership and the IT project success criteria. Then, it would be concluded that the null hypobook for (RQ1) would be rejected. On the other hand, if the indirect effect (a_1*b_1) confidence intervals contain a zero, then the null hypobook for (RQ1) would fail to be rejected. If the null hypobook is rejected, trust in leaders would explain the relationship between servant leadership and project management success. This process will then be repeated for the criterion variables of results success (RQ2) using (Y_2) and perception success (RQ3) using (Y_3). A summary of the results will be presented in

Chapter 4, and further discussion and conclusion will be provided in Chapter 5.

Ethical Considerations

Research ethics are crucial, and this study was no exception. This quantitative research adhered to the elements outlined in the Belmont Report, which outlines the three governing research principles for conducting research with human subjects: respect for persons, beneficence, and justice (Miracle, 2016). When expressed as requirements, these three factors are informed consent, risk/benefit analysis, and selection of research participants (U.S. Department of Health & Human Services, 1979). This study gathered data from human subjects, requiring careful planning to ensure the participants are granted these ethical factors within the proposal (Kaewkungwal & Adams, 2019), along with fair and equal treatment.

Informed consent was provided before obtaining research or other data. Participant recruitment did not begin before obtaining GCU IRB approval. The informed consent form (Appendix D) was presented to each participant. This consent form contains the participant's rights and essential research information, allowing the participants to consent to participate in the research voluntarily by selecting "I agree" in the survey and can opt-out at any time.

Additional measures were taken to ensure the rights and well-being of the study participants. The participants' rights and well-being were ensured, and their autonomy was respected, as no identifiable information was included in the data collection. No other personal identifiers or internet protocol addresses (IPs) were included in the survey data procedures through Qualtrics© survey platform and service. Data collection adhered to the Data Protection Act of 1998 to ensure participant rights were strictly followed. This adherence ensures participant anonymity, prevents data loss, and maintains data security (Hart et al., 2016). The data will be stored in the LDP AQR reviewer folder for sharing with the University, committee, or other relevant approved parties and an external hard drive. The external hard drive is encrypted, fingerprint-secured, and passwordprotected. The external hard drive will be stored in a safe for three years, according to GCU data storage policy, after which the external hard drive will be purged and returned to the original factory settings, rendering any possible data unrecoverable and unusable (Scope et al., 2022).

The final research ethical element of the Belmont Report is the subject selection process. The selection of the target population included the local PMI Chapter (PMIPHX.org). All processes and approvals for GCU are officially captured, to include the approval from the PMI (Appendix B). All proper procedures were followed using the PMI process (Appendix B). The target populations for each research plan were approved by GCU IRB and were provided with a Qualtrics© survey link that the professional service platform managed. There was no direct contact between the participants and the researcher at any time during the study, as it was administered through the Qualtrics© platform, ensuring and maintaining the anonymity of the participants. Further, this study did not involve vulnerable populations per Federal regulations and GCU IRB standards.

Assumptions and Delimitations

Assumptions

An assumption is something beyond the researcher's control. If these assumptions are absent, the research could be deemed meaningless (Simon & Goes, 2018). Assumptions in research must be reasonable and likely actual, or the study should not proceed (Simon & Goes, 2018). These assumptions will cover the research's methodological, ontological, epistemological, axiological, and rhetorical aspects

(Sukamolson, 2007). The following assumptions apply to this research:

1. Participants in the survey are assumed to respond truthfully. This assumption is reasonable as participants have no incentive to deceive and are expected to answer honestly. The instruments used are valid and reliable based on previous studies. If participants are intentionally

or unintentionally deceptive, the results could be invalid as the variable measurements may not be accurate or reliable.

2. Any potential biases from the researcher, committee, AQR review, IRB, or any other relevant party are assumed not to influence the research findings. This assumption is reasonable as none of these parties will participate in the study, and all collected data will adhere to the rigorous processes and ethical guidelines of GCU IRB.

3. The researcher, committee members, and all other relevant parties are assumed to remain independent of the participants completing the survey. This assumption is reasonable as the surveys will be distributed using online collection tools, preventing interaction with the participants before, during, or after the survey. The participants remain anonymous.

Furthermore, the data analysis for this study was checked for the validity and reliability of each variable before determining any results. Any inaccuracies are openly and honestly discussed and presented in Chapters 4 and 5.

Delimitations

Delimitations are factors that narrow the scope of a study and set its boundaries

(Simon & Goes, 2018). Unlike assumptions, researchers have control over delimitations. Delimitations are crucial for research as they guide the scope and make the study manageable (Theofanidis & Fountouki, 2018). However, they can also restrict the applicability and generalizability of the results. The delimitations of this study include:

1. This study examines three specific theoretical models/instruments, which may limit the applicability of the findings to other models measuring the same constructs. To lessen the impact of this delimitation, the researcher should provide a detailed explanation for using each model and interpret the study results accurately in terms of these models.

2. The study uses convenience sampling instead of randomized sampling. This delimitation could restrict the generalizability of the findings, as the sample might not represent the larger population. To counteract

this delimitation, the researcher should include a more diverse population in the study and strive for the largest sample size possible to increase generalizability. This delimitation should also be mentioned in the future recommendations section in Chapter 5, as randomized sampling would enhance generalizability more than convenience sampling.

3. The study focuses on the mediating effects of 'trust in leaders'. It does not consider other potential mediators, such as organizational effectiveness, team potency, or psychological safety. Also, no moderating variables were used in this study. This delimitation will be mentioned in Chapter 5 as a suggestion for future research.

4. The study is delimited to adult IT project team members within the United States who have been a part of an IT project team in the last three years. The findings might not be relevant to projects in other industries or IT projects within other countries. To lessen this delimitation, the researcher could compare results from different project types across different cultures. This study will be noted as a limitation and discussed as a potential future research recommendation. Additionally, this could limit the generalizability of the study.

Summary

The purpose of this quantitative correlational predictive study was to examine if, or to what extent, trust in leaders mediates the relationship between servant leadership and IT project success dimensions of project management success, perception success, and result success within technology project teams in the United States. The research employs quantitative methodology and a correlational predictive design, which is deemed the most suitable approach to address the research questions. Furthermore, this study employs a quantitative methodology that uses deductive reasoning and statistical analysis evaluate the research questions (Asenahabi, 2019) and to investigate the correlational relationship between variables (Hamida Bibi et al., 2022). This rationale and alignment form the appropriate framework for this research, as established in this chapter.

The target population for this study included adult IT project team members (18 years and older) based in the United States, estimated to be over 2.5 million individuals. This population is crucial to answering the three research questions for this study as they provide the data necessary to address the foundational gap this study represents. The survey consists of demographic and organizational questions and three valid and reliable instruments: SL-7 (Liden et al., 2015), TIL (Podsakoff et al., 1990), and ITPS dimensions (Harwardt, 2018). According to the G*power calculation and additional buffers for attrition and potentially missing data, the appropriate sample size to adequately answer the research questions is 89 participants. Data collected from the sample were captured online using the Qualtrics© survey platform. The participants received an informed consent page before entering the survey phase, following all GCU IRB policies and procedures for research engagement with human participants. This was conducted before entering the survey's response portion, ensuring the fundamental principles of respect, justice, and beneficence of the Belmont Report are followed (Miracle, 2016). The survey consisted of five demographic questions, four organizational demographic questions, and a 20item aggregated instrumentation survey. This collected data is used to understand the diversity and breadth of the sample and further view the measures of central tendency and variance of the variables measured.

Once the data is cleaned and reviewed, it will be tested for assumptions, for mediation analyses, it is most appropriate to apply the same assumptions as a multiple linear regression analysis (Abu-Bader & Jones, 2021). After this, the first of three mediation analyses will be conducted using the Hayes (2018) PROCESS macro v4.3 for SPSS v29. The output of these three mediation analyses will help answer the three research questions and determine whether the associated null hypotheses are rejected. Furthermore, collected data will be held for three years on an externally encrypted hard drive, according to GCU storage policy standards. Moreover, the data will be destroyed, as Scope et al. (2022) laid out, by purging the data through a factory reset.

In Chapter 4, the processes and procedures planned in Chapter 3 were used to run the data analysis using actual participant data after IRB approvals. This is presented using written and table formats, providing detailed information on the data collected for this study. This will precede Chapter 5, in which a discussion of the results and conclusions is presented.

Chapter 4: Data Analysis and Results

Introduction

The purpose of this quantitative correlational predictive study is to examine to what extent trust in leaders mediates the relationship between servant leadership and the IT project success dimensions of project management success, perception success, and results success within technology project team members in the United States. As IT project teams face increasing complexity and leadership challenges, understanding the role of servant leadership and trust in leaders is critical for improving project outcomes. This study examines these relationships to provide insights that may inform leadership practices and contribute to IT project success. Data were gathered from adult IT project team members from across the United States using the Qualtrics© platform. Likert-type measurement scales were used to assess servant leadership, trust in leaders, and IT project success dimensions. The survey was distributed through use of paid Qualtrics© panels, and responses were analyzed to examine the relationships among the study variables. This study investigated three research questions to determine whether trust in leaders mediates the relationship between servant leadership and the three dimensions of
IT project success.

Survey data were obtained using three validated and reliable instruments administered through the Qualtrics© survey platform. It utilized a convenience sample of 142 adult IT project team members who had participated in an IT project team within the past three years in the United States. Participants also provided demographic data, including personal factors (age, gender, educational qualifications, professional experience, and project experience) and organizational-level variables (business sector, employment status as a contractor or full-time employee, employer size, and current management level). The research questions and hypotheses were structured to align with the three study variables: servant leadership, trust in leaders, and the three dimensions of IT project success (project management success, perception success, and result success). Each variable was measured using Likert scales and analyzed using descriptive statistics at both individual and organizational levels. Inferential statistics were used in OLS regression analysis to evaluate the study hypotheses.

To ensure clarity and accessibility, the results of this study are thoroughly presented in the following sections, beginning with data preparation, assumption testing, descriptive statistics, inferential statistical analysis, and study limitations. The study findings are presented using tables, graphs, figures, and charts, followed by an in-depth statistical analysis to address the research questions and hypotheses:

RQ1: Does trust in leaders mediate the relationship between servant leadership and project management success?

$H1_0$: Trust in leaders does not significantly mediate the relationship between servant leadership and project management success.

$H1_a$: Trust in leaders does significantly mediate the relationship between servant leadership and project management success.

RQ2: Does trust in leaders mediate the relationship between servant leadership and perception success?

$H2_0$: Trust in leaders does not significantly mediate the relationship between servant leadership and perception success.

$H2_a$: Trust in leaders does significantly mediate the relationship between servant leadership and perception success.

RQ3: Does trust in leaders mediate the relationship between servant leadership and result success?

$H3_0$: Trust in leaders does not significantly mediate the relationship between servant leadership and result success.

$H3_a$: Trust in leaders does significantly mediate the relationship between servant leadership and result success.

Important Changes and Updates

The original proposal underwent minimal changes. The first change involved managing outliers. Seven standard multiple regressions were conducted for assumption testing due to the three criterion variables and two predictor relationships (servant leadership and trust in leaders). Three outliers exceeded the ±3 standard deviation of the mean threshold (Osborne & Overbay, 2004), which the standardized residual values for the three outliers were –3.267, –3.134, and 3.206, however Cook's distance (< 1.0) and leverage calculations (< 0.2) confirmed that these outliers were within tolerance and did not require removal (Laerd Statistics, 2022). As recommended by Snee (1983), multiple diagnostics should be used when evaluating outliers rather than relying solely on standardized residuals. Therefore, these potential outliers did not negatively affect the results and were retained in the final dataset.

The second change involved an update to the original sampling plan. This change did not result from modifications to the plans but from the inability to aggregate all three plans. After 30 days, Plans A and B yielded 21 valid survey responses. Due to the low response rate, reliance on Plan C (Qualtrics© panels) became necessary. As a result, recruitment Plans A and B were completely removed from the data collection process approved by IRB. Moreover, the 21 responses obtained from Plans A and B were excluded from the final dataset due to the inability to verify that duplicate participants were not present in either source. This exclusion was based on the limitation that Qualtrics© did not collect IP addresses, preventing the identification and removal of potential duplicate entries. To preserve the integrity of the sample and reduce the risk of response bias, only the data collected through the Qualtrics panels ($N = 142$) were retained for the analysis. Although this was not a deviation from the proposal, these changes for Plans A and B are addressed within this chapter and will also be discussed in the study limitations section. The following section discusses data preparation, assumption testing, descriptive statistics, and the presentation of study findings and limitations.

Preparation of Raw Data for Analysis and Tests of Assumptions

Preparation of Raw Data for Analysis

First, the raw data was reviewed within the Qualtrics© platform. This initial review was conducted prior to downloading the CSV file for cleaning and preparation. The Qualtrics© team configured the survey to allow only fully completed responses to be included ensuring that incomplete data were not recorded. After data collection, the dataset was examined for missing values, outliers, and entry errors. A total of 142 completed surveys were obtained through Qualtrics© internal panels. No missing or erroneous data were identified. This final sample size (N = 142) exceeds the minimum required sample size of (n = 68), as determined by G*Power analysis. The dataset was then exported as a CSV file, where responses were converted into numeric values for statistical analysis. Then the single reverse-coded item for trust in leaders was recalculated, and survey responses were scored and aggregated according to the scoring guides for each instrument. This data was then input into the SPSS v29 program for assumption testing and descriptive and inferential statistical analysis.

Tests of Assumptions for Multiple Linear Regression

Independence of Observations. The assumption of independence of observations was assessed using the Durbin-Watson test in SPSS v29 to detect potential autocorrelation or serial correlation in the data. According to Laerd Statistics (2022), Durbin-Watson values range from 0 to 4, with a target value of approximately 2, indicating no significant autocorrelation. As summarized in Table 4, all Durbin-Watson values are within the acceptable range, confirming that the assumption of independence of residuals for OLS regression was met.

Table 4

Independence of Observations Assumptions

Regression Path	Durbin-Watson Test
Servant Leadership and Project Management Success	2.218
Servant Leadership and Perception Success	2.111
Servant Leadership and Result Success	2.159
Trust in Leaders and Project Management Success	2.003
Trust in Leaders and Perception Success	2.143
Trust in Leaders and Result Success	1.975
Servant Leadership and Trust in Leaders	2.026

Test for Outliers. This assumption was reviewed using the casewise diagnostics output table in SPSS v29. Outliers were assessed case by case to determine whether they resulted from entry errors, missing data, or genuine variability (Vinisha & Sujihelen, 2022). Three data points (19, 48, and 102) exceeded the ±3 standard deviation threshold, commonly used in multiple regression assumption testing (Laerd Statistics, 2022). However, an analysis of Cook's distance and leverage values indicated that these outliers were within tolerance and did not require removal. A leverage value below 0.2 supports keeping a data point and should be considered before evaluating Cook's Distance (Laerd Statistics, 2022). If Cook's Distance exceeds 1.0, the high-influence point is removed, and all assumptions are retested (Laerd Statistics, 2022). All three data points met Cook's distance and leverage criteria. Therefore, these three data points were retained in the data set. Therefore, the assumption of having no significant outliers was met.

Linearity. The assumption of linearity was assessed using visual inspection of scatterplots, for each regression path. According to Laerd Statistics (2022), a linear relationship must be present for regression analysis, whether positive, negative, or with a zero slope. An examination of the scatterplots indicated a linear relationship, as evidenced by a relatively flat or zero slope, suggesting no significant curvature in the data. Figures 4 through 10 in below present these findings. Therefore, the assumption of linearity was met.

Figure 4

Scatterplot of Servant Leadership and Project Management Success

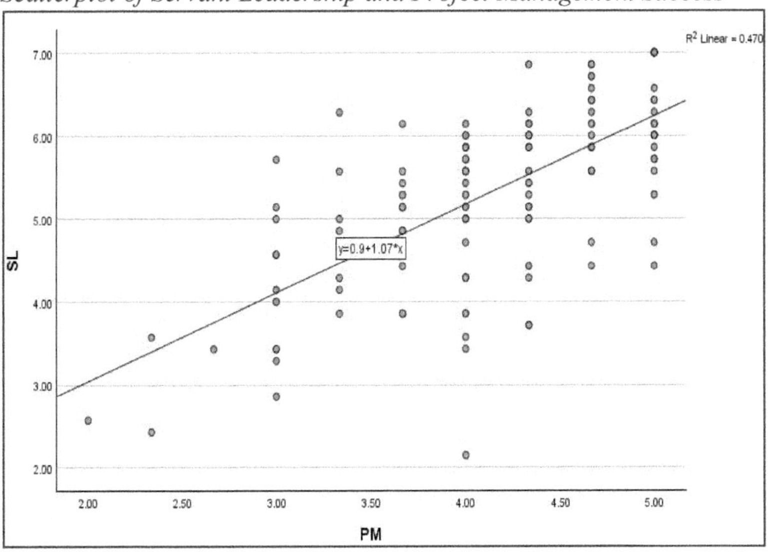

Figure 5

Scatterplot of Servant Leadership and Perception Success

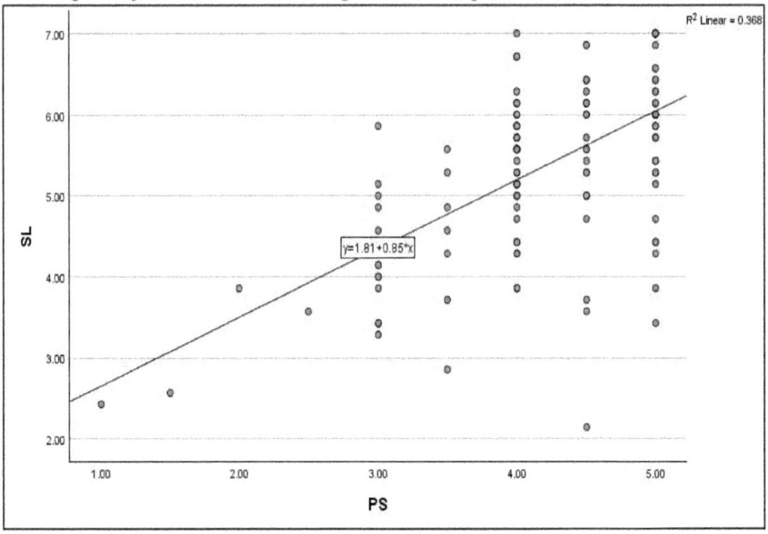

Figure 6

Scatterplot of Servant Leadership and Result Success

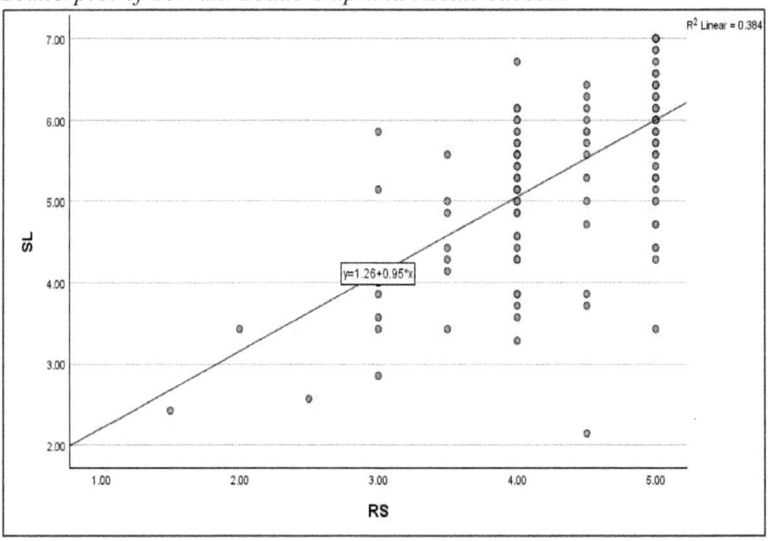

Figure 7

Scatterplot of Servant Leadership and Trust in Leaders

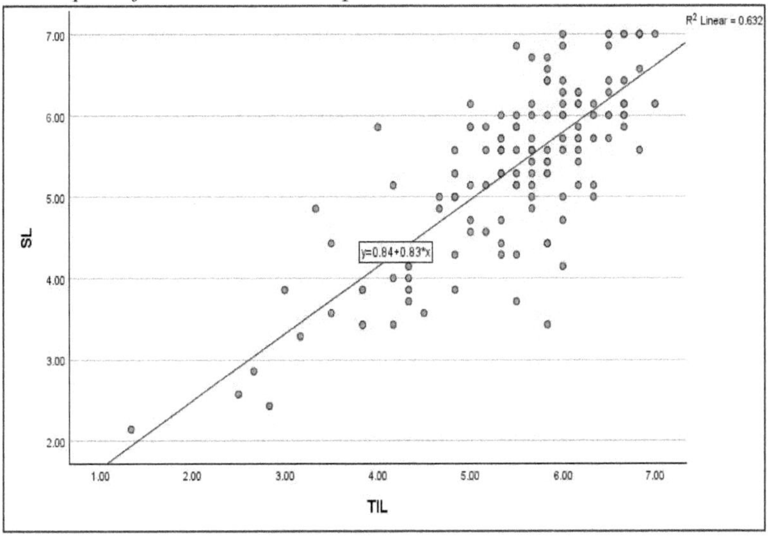

Figure 8

Scatterplot of Trust in Leaders and Project Management Success

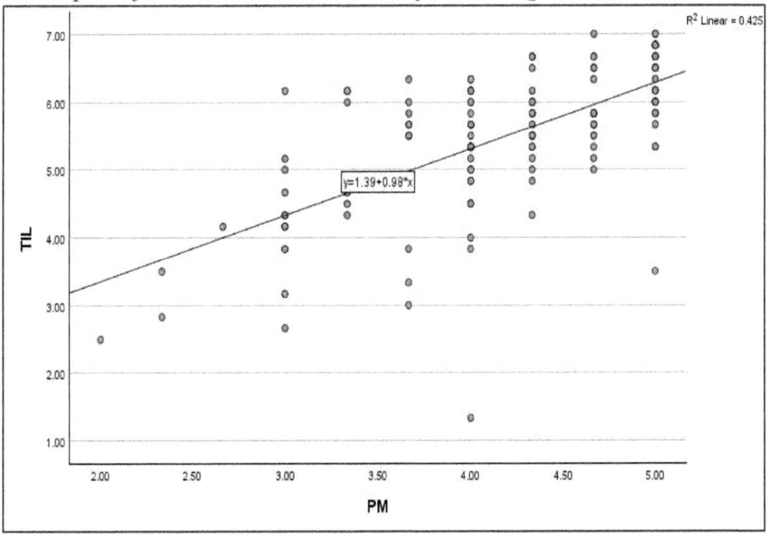

Figure 9

Scatterplot of Trust in Leaders and Perception Success

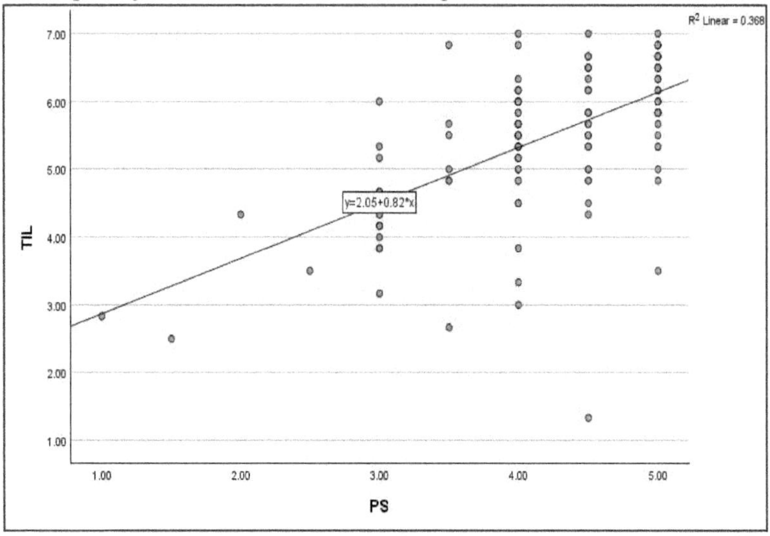

Figure 10

Scatterplot of Trust in Leaders and Result Success

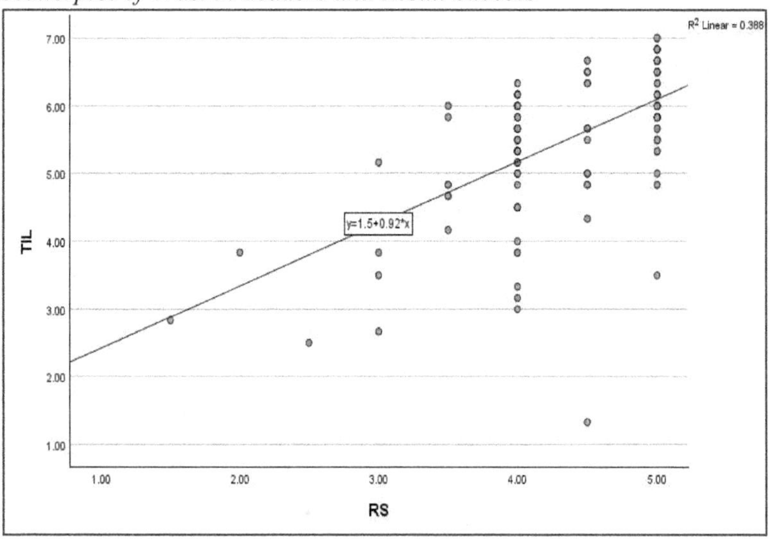

Homoscedasticity. This assumption, also known as constancy of variance, was assessed through visual inspection of a plot of standardized residuals versus unstandardized predicted values (Laerd Statistics, 2022).

These are illustrated in Figures 11 through 17 below. For homoscedasticity to be met, the residuals should be evenly distributed across all levels of predicted values without forming a funnel or fan shape (Laerd Statistics, 2022). Inspection of the residual plot showed no visible pattern or clustering, displaying an equal spacing of the data. Therefore, this assumption was met.

R

Figure 11

Scatterplot of esiduals of Servant Leadership and Project Management Success

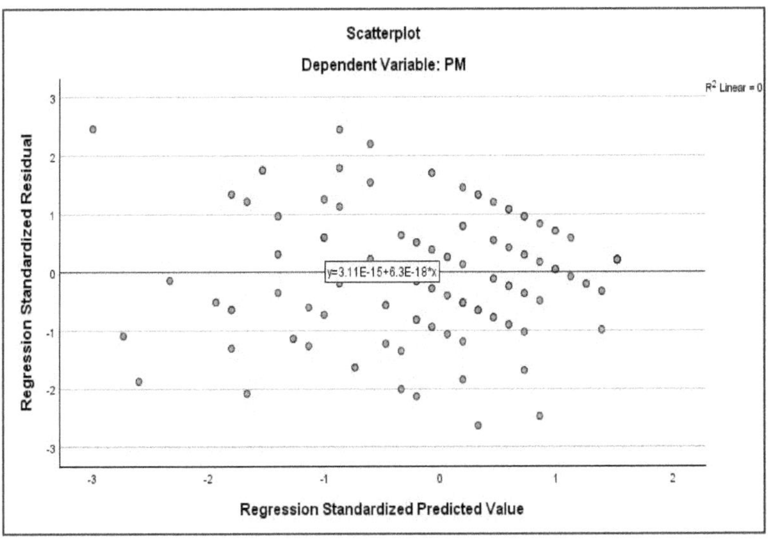

Figure 12

Scatterplot of Residuals of Servant Leadership and Perception Success

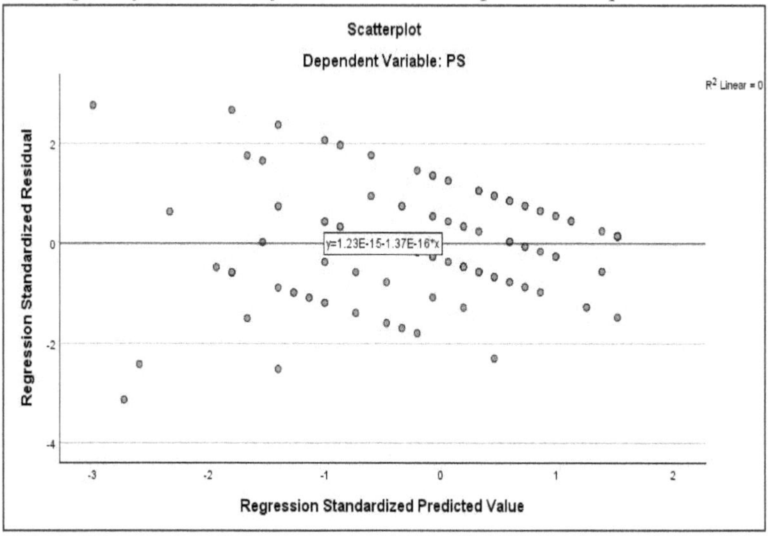

Figure 13

Scatterplot of esiduals of Servant Leadership and Result Success

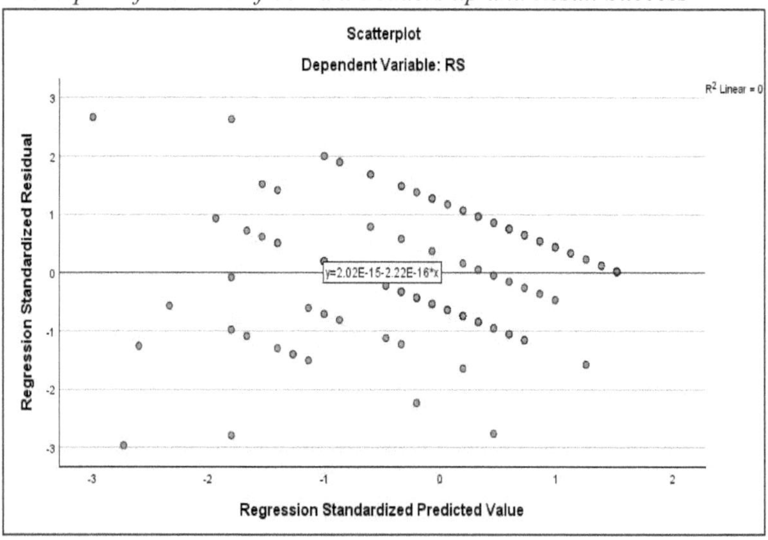

R

Figure 14

Scatterplot of Residuals of Servant Leadership and Trust in Leaders

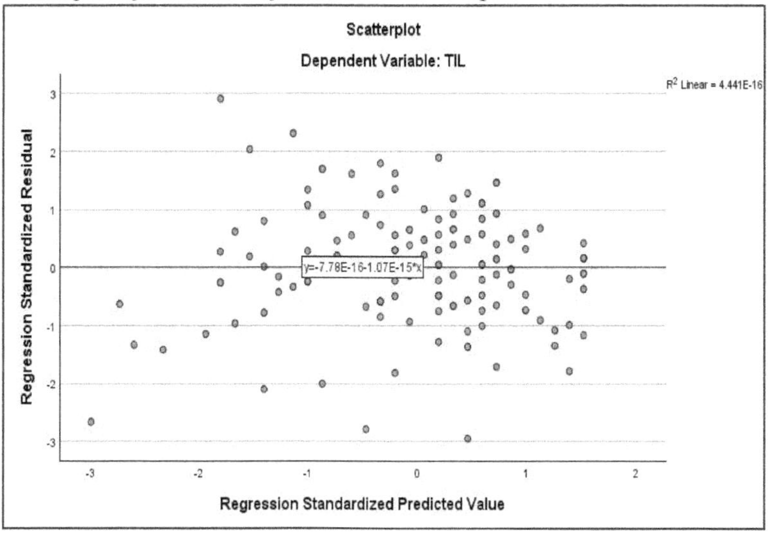

Figure 15

Scatterplot of esiduals of Trust in Leaders and Project Management Success

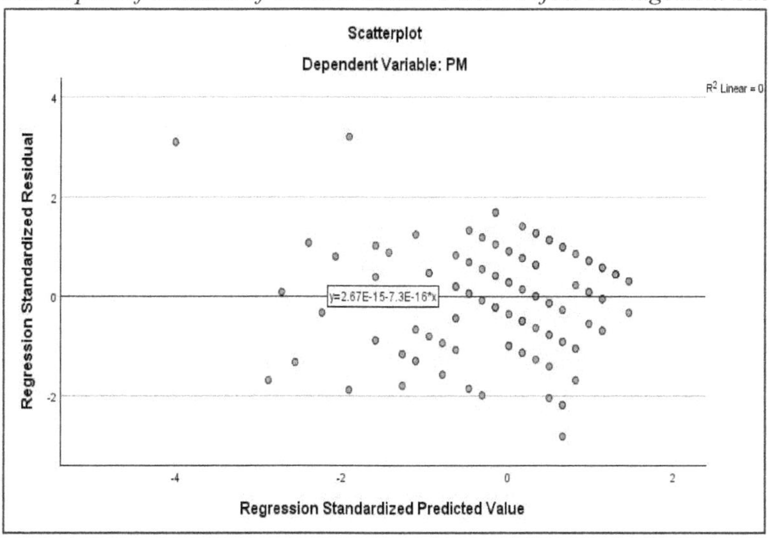

Figure 16

Scatterplot of Residuals of Trust in Leaders and Perception Success

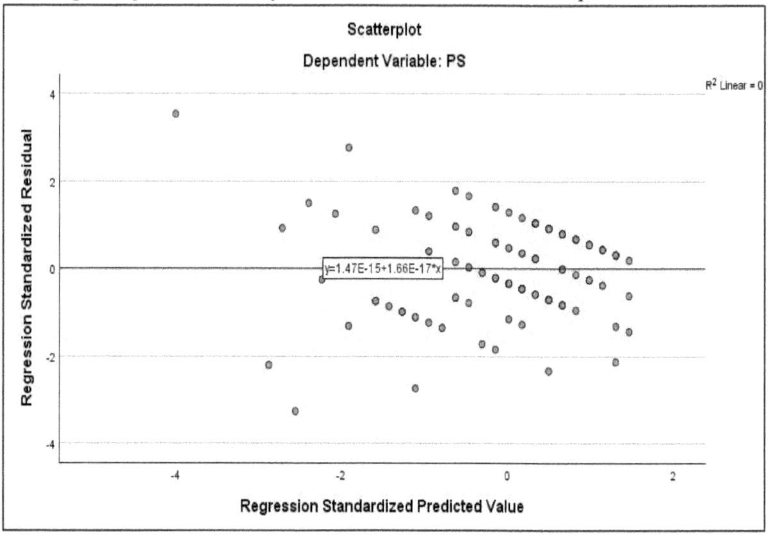

Figure 17

Scatterplot of esiduals of Trust in Leaders and Result Success

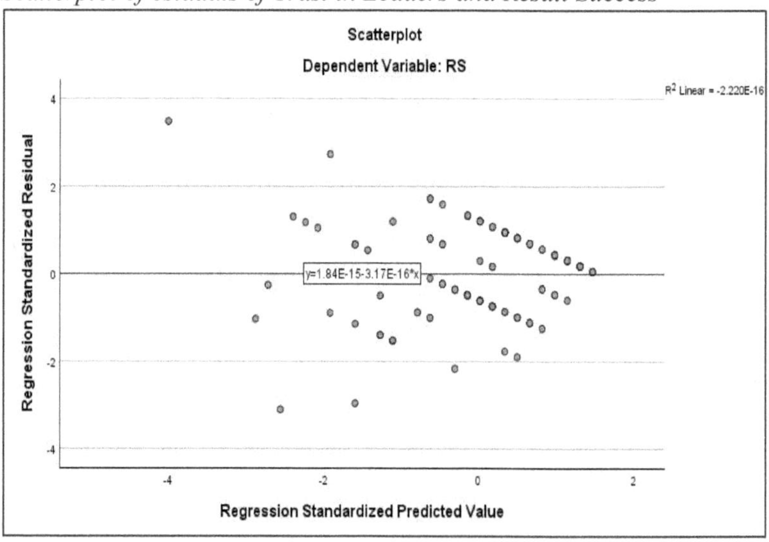

R

Normality of Residuals. This assumption requires that residuals be normally distributed, which can be assessed through visual inspection of a histogram and a normal P-P plot (Laerd Statistics, 2022). This study used visual inspections of a histogram and normal P-P plot to evaluate normality. The histograms and P-P plots (Figures 18 through 31) indicate that all regression models exhibit approximate normality based on visual inspection. Normality was further assessed using skewness and kurtosis statistics. Skewness values ranged from –0.679 to –1.184, and kurtosis values from 0.004 to 2.038, all within acceptable ranges of ±2 for skewness and ±7 for kurtosis (Blanca et al., 2012).

Therefore, this assumption was met for OLS regression analysis.

Figure 18

Normal P P Plot of Servant Leadership and Project Management Success

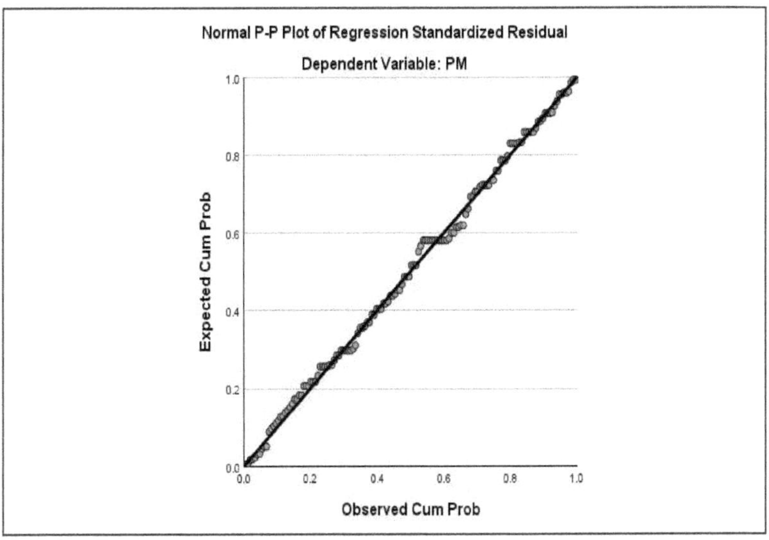

Figure 19

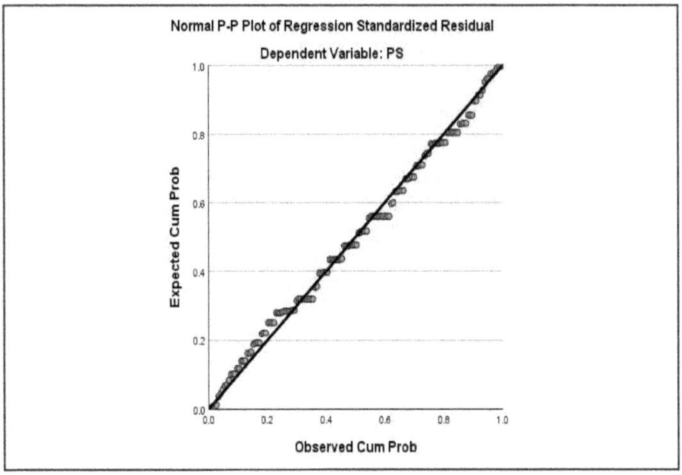

Normal P-P Plot of Servant Leadership and Perception Success

Figure 20

Normal P P Plot of Servant Leadership and Result Success

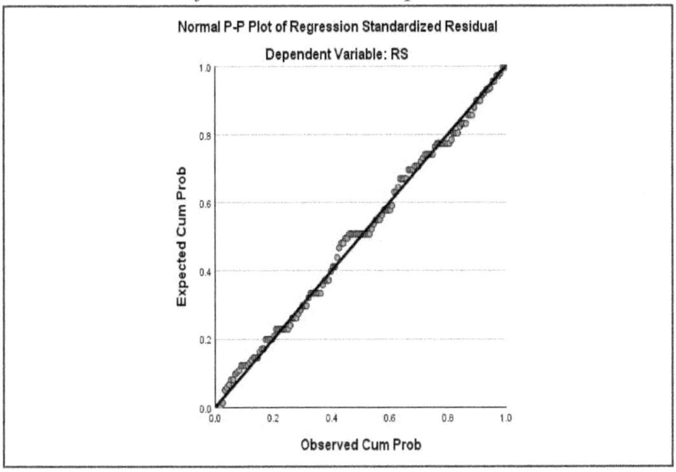

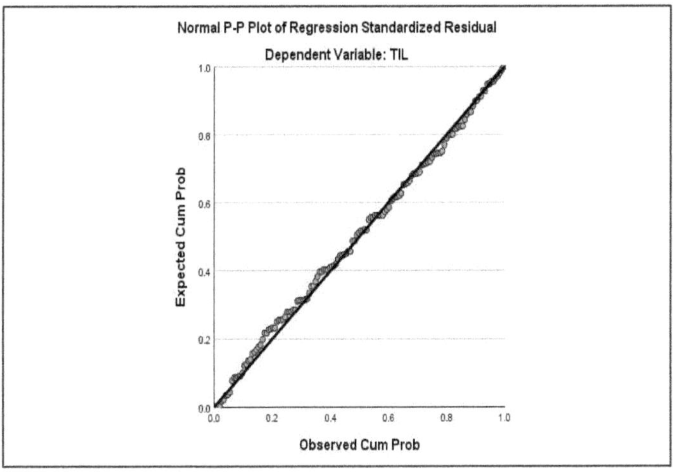

Figure 21

Normal P-P Plot of Servant Leadership and Trust in Leaders

-

Figure 22

Normal P P Plot of Trust in Leaders and Project Management Success

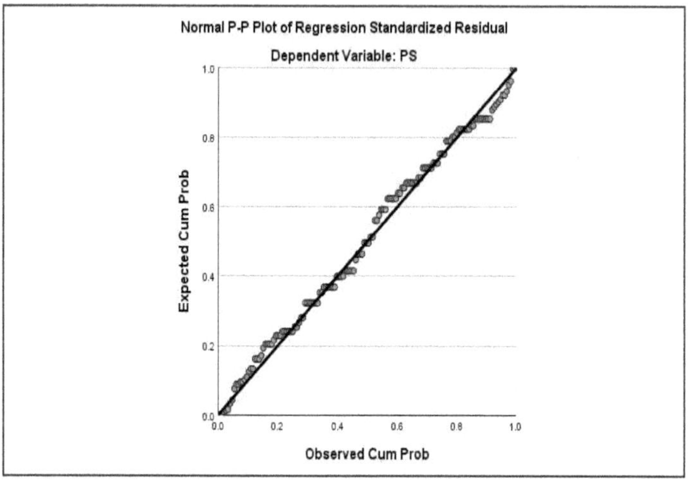

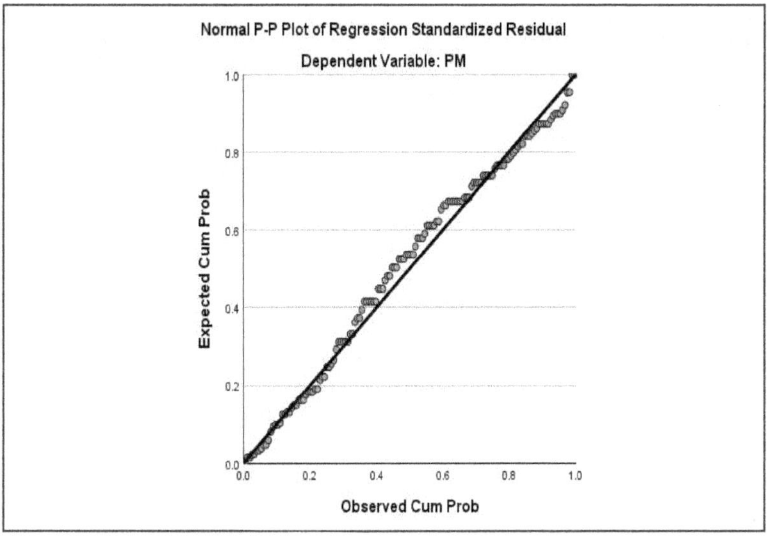

Figure 23

Normal P-P Plot of Trust in Leaders and Perception Success

Figure 24

-

Normal P P Plot of Trust in Leaders and Result Success

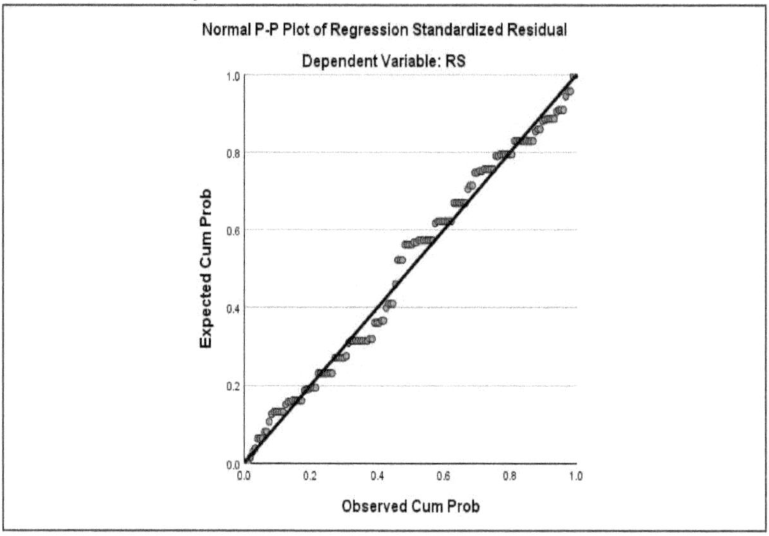

Figure 25

Histogram of Servant Leadership and Project Management Success

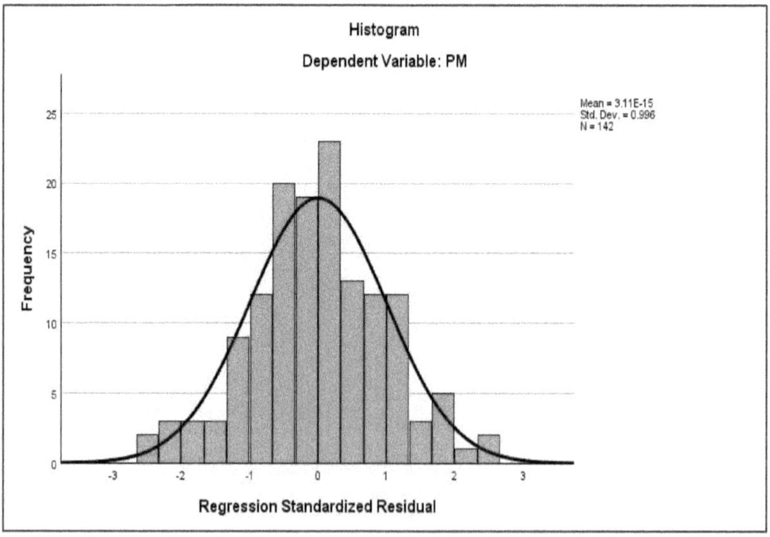

Figure 26

Histogram of Servant Leadership and Perception Success

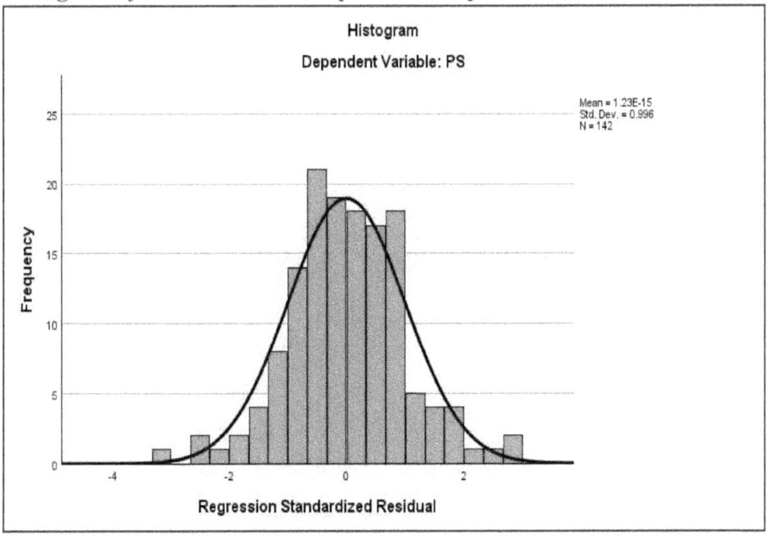

Figure 27

Histogram of Servant Leadership and Result Success

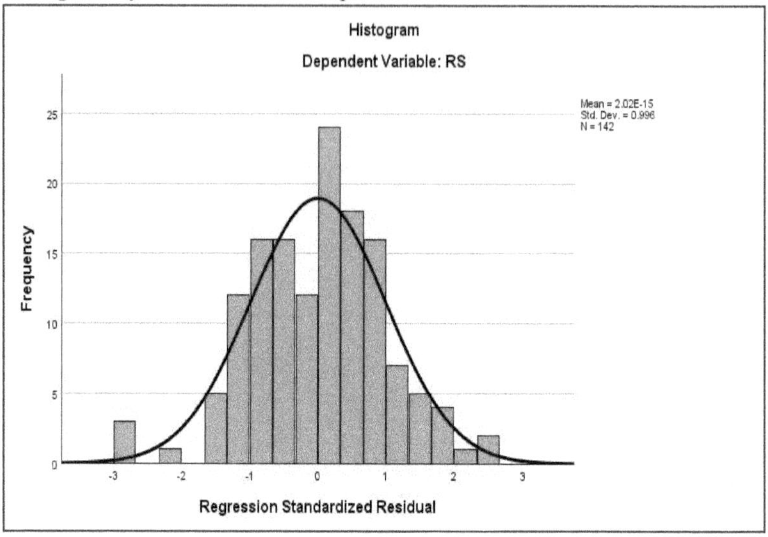

Figure 28

Histogram of Servant Leadership and Trust in Leaders

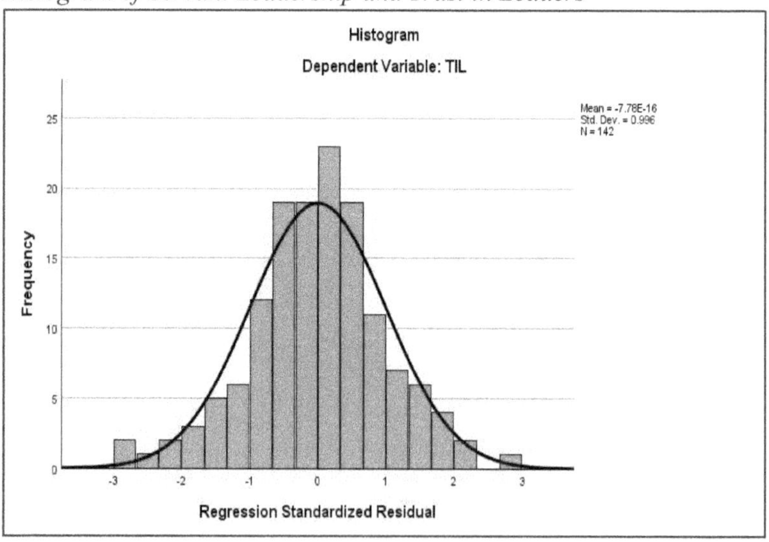

Figure 29

Histogram of Trust in Leaders and Project Management Success

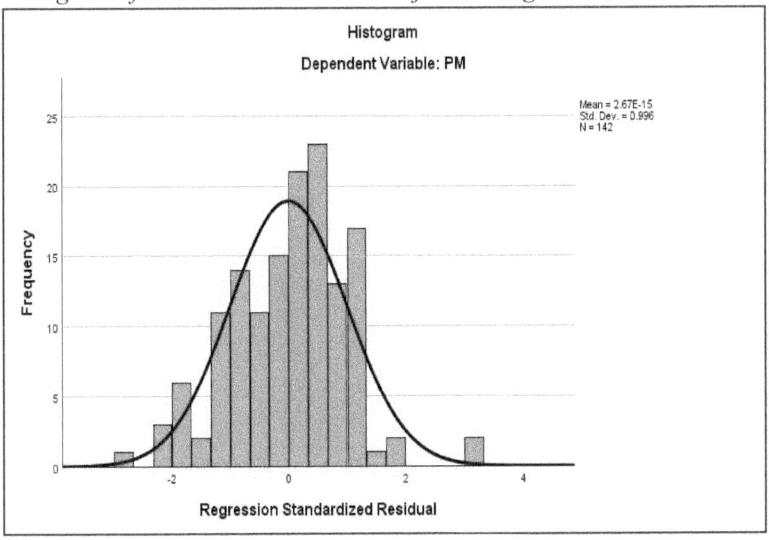

Figure 30

Histogram of Trust in Leaders and Perception Success

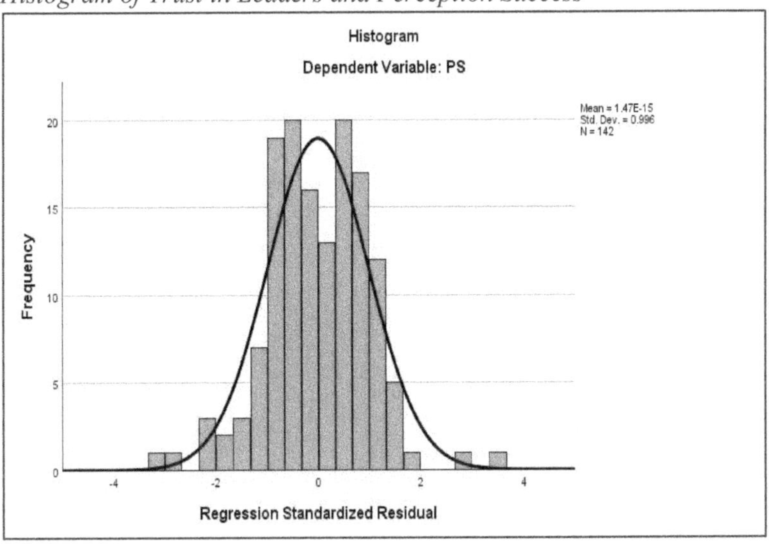

Figure 31

Histogram of Trust in Leaders and Result Success

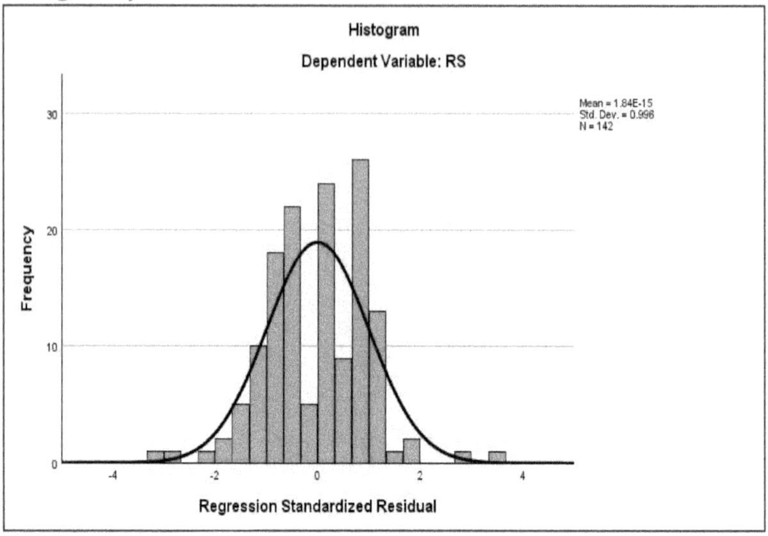

Multicollinearity. This assumption requires that predictor variables not be highly correlated with each other (Laerd Statistics, 2022). Multicollinearity was assessed by examining the variance inflation factor (VIF) (Kyriazos & Poga, 2023), where all values must be below 5 to meet the assumption (Laerd Statistics, 2022). For this study, the VIF values ranged from 1.000 to 2.721, below the threshold of 5 for each relationship tested, indicating no multicollinearity issues. Therefore, this assumption was met.

Summary. The study data was reviewed in the Qualtrics© platform prior to downloading to ensure the data collection was completed as per requirements and sample size. The data set was then downloaded using a CSV file copied and pasted into a Microsoft Excel file. All study data was then appropriately cleaned, including input errors, missing data, or potential entry errors. Each inconsistency was addressed on a case-by-case basis and no data points were removed. All multiple linear regression assumptions were met, supporting the use of OLS regression analysis for this study. Therefore, all assumptions for OLS regression analysis were satisfied, and the research was conducted as planned. As such, no non-parametric test was required for this research.

Descriptive Findings

Before conducting inferential statistical analysis, it is crucial to understand the characteristics of the variables to ensure the data being evaluated is representative of the population. Descriptive statistics summarize data patterns and distribution characteristics. Tables 5 and 6 below provide demographic information about the sample population, which includes individual and organizational breakdowns. Table 7 presents the means, medians, modes, standard deviations, variances, skewness, and kurtosis for each of the study variables, and these findings are discussed in the study variable descriptives below.

Demographics

The target population for this study consisted of adult individuals involved in IT project teams in the United States. This population has many diverse professional experiences and educational backgrounds, which were considerations provided in the survey. Survey participants ranged in gender, skilled work experience, and IT project experience, ensuring that the sample population represented individuals with a broad range of characteristics.

To be included in the study, participants must have been at least 18 years of age and had been a member of an IT project within the last three years. Individuals who did not meet these criteria were excluded from participation to ensure the relevancy of the data collected. A total of ($N = 142$) participants were included in the final sample. Descriptive statistics for the sample demographics are provided below, which offers a demographic overview of the sample population. Tables 8 and 9 display the breakdowns in individual and organizational demographics.

Individual Demographics. The sample included 68% male participants and 32% female participants. No participants identified as "Other" or preferred not to answer. The largest group ($n = 63$, 45%) of respondents had a bachelor's degree, followed by ($n = 43$, 30%) with a master's degree, with only ($n = 6$, 4%) having a doctorate. For professional experience, the largest group of respondents ($n = 53$, 37%) had between 6 and 15 years of professional experience, with the smallest group representing 5 years or less ($n = 8$, 6%) of experience. The respondents were relatively experienced in IT projects, with ($n = 52$, 37%) having 6 to 10 years of IT project experience, and 23% with 11 to 20 years, while ($n = 13$, 9%) had more than 31 years of IT project experience. Table 5 provides further detail on these individual demographics below.

Table 5

Individual Demographics

Demographic	Frequency	Percentage
Gender		
Male	97	68%
Female	45	32%
Other/Prefer not to answer	0	0%

Highest Level of Education		
High School	14	10%
Professional Certification	15	11%
Bachelors	63	45%
Masters	43	30%
Doctorate	6	4%
Professional Work Experience	8	
5 years or less		6%
6 to 15 years	53	37%
16 to 25 years	36	25%
26 to 35 years	18	13%
36 years or more	27	19%
IT Project Experience		
5 years or less	28	20%
6 to 10 years	52	37%
11 to 20 years	33	23%
21 to 30 years	16	11%
31 years or more	13	9%

Organizational Demographics. The sample consisted of 38 participants (27%) who were contractors, while 104 participants (73%) were full-time employees. For the industry sector question, the largest group, 93 participants (65%), worked in the IT and ecommerce sector, followed by 10 participants (7%) in health and social services, with smaller percentages in banking, insurance, media, and other sectors. Most participants (n = 37, 26%) worked in organizations with 251–1,000 employees, followed by 31 participants (22%) in companies with 1,001–10,000 employees. Smaller organizations of 10 employees or fewer accounted for 13 participants (9%). Many participants, 49 (35%), were in senior management roles, followed by

44 (31%) in middle management, 20 (14%) in first-line management, and 29 (20%) who were non-managers. Table 6 further demonstrates these organizational demographic breakdowns.

Table 6

Organizational Demographics

Demographic	Frequency	Percentage
Contractor? Yes	38	27%
No	104	73%
Industry Sector		
Bank and Insurance	5	4%
Service	2	1%
Media	1	1%
IT and e-Commerce	93	65%
Health and Social Services	10	7%
Trade and Distribution	3	2%
Administration and Public Services	3	2%
Organizational Size		
10 employees or less	13	9%
11 to 50 employees	14	10%
51 to 250 employees	20	14%
251 to 1,000 employees	37	26%
1,001 to 10,000 employees	31	22%
More than 10,000 employees	27	19%
Current Management Level		
First-line Management	20	14%
Middle Management	44	31%
Senior Management	49	35%
Non-manager	29	20%

Comparison with Target Population. Based on the target population, the sample appears representative across key characteristics like gender, education, and experience.

The gender breakdown and educational levels of the sample are consistent with the general population of IT project team members, focusing on IT and eCommerce industry sectors and organizational size, management levels, and contracting opportunities.

Study Variable Descriptives

Servant Leadership. The servant Leadership variable had a mean of 5.363, indicating respondents agreed with the questions about servant leadership behaviors. The standard deviation of 1.076 shows that most participants had similar responses. The skewness of –0.629 indicates a slight leftward skew, reflecting that some responses were lower than the majority. The kurtosis of 0.041 suggests a normal distribution.

Trust in Leaders. The trust in leaders variable had a mean of 5.480, showing that respondents agreed with the statements reflecting trust in their leaders. The standard deviation of 1.033 indicates there is not a lot of distribution in the responses. While the skewness of –1.129 suggests a leftward skew, meaning more respondents had a favorable view of trust in their leaders. The kurtosis of 1.622 indicates a peaked distribution, showing that responses were grouped around the mean.

Project Management Success. The project management success dimension had a mean of 4.176, indicating that respondents were optimistic about the short-term success of their projects. The standard deviation 2.00

shows that responses were spread out, with a balance of positive and negative views. The skewness of –0.679 and negative kurtosis of –1.184 suggest that the data was skewed and flatter, with significant response variance.

Perception Success. In reviewing the perception success dimension, or mediumterm success, the mean of 4.197 shows a positive perception of success for the mediumterm duration of a project. The standard deviation of 1.50 shows a broad distribution with uneven success ratings. The skewness of –1.047 indicates that many respondents viewed the projects positively. The kurtosis of –2.038 shows a flatter distribution with less response variation.

Result Success. The result success dimension, or long-term success, had a mean of 4.328, indicating that respondents perceived their project results as successful. The standard deviation of 0.769 shows that responses were close to the mean. The skewness of –0.493 suggests a mild leftward skew, and the kurtosis of 1.443 indicates a peak in the data, with most responses around the mean.

Summary. The descriptive statistics indicate positive participant perceptions of servant leadership, trust in leaders, project management success, perception success, and result success. The kurtosis for Perception Success showed more fluctuation in responses. The skewness results suggest that the data approximate a normal distribution, with a leftward skew, indicating a more positive view of all the study variables. The descriptive statistic results demonstrate that the sample represents the population and is suitable for inferential analysis.

Table 7

Descriptive Statistics

Variable	*N*	*Mean*	*Median*	*Mode*	*Min*	*Max*	*Std. Deviation*	*Variance*	*Skewness*	*Kurtosis*
Servant Leadership	142	5.363	5.571	5.57	2.14	7.00	1.076	1.157	–.629	.041
Trust in Leaders	142	5.480	5.667	5.83	1.33	7.00	1.036	1.074	–1.129	1.622
Project Management Success	142	4.176	4.333	4.00	2.00	5.00	.691	.477	–.679	.004
Perception Success	142	4.197	4.000	4.00	1.00	5.00	.769	.592	–1.184	2.038
Result Success	142	4.328	4.500	5.00	1.50	5.00	.702	.493	–1.047	1.443

Reliability of Scale Variables. The reliability analysis was conducted using Cronbach's alpha to assess the internal consistency of the study variables. Table 8 summarizes the results. Cronbach's alpha coefficients indicate acceptable reliability for all instruments, confirming that no variables required removal. Additionally, all coefficients align with the reliability ranges reported in current research for each instrument.

Table 8

Reliability Statistics – Cronbach's Alpha (N = 142)

Instrument	Range from Current Research	Current Study
Servant leadership (SL)	.74 – .95	.862
Trust in Leaders (TIL)	.71 – .93	.803
Project Management Success (PM)	.921	.813
Perception Success (PS)	.865	.822
Result Success (RS)	.850	.805

Post-Hoc Power Analysis. A post-hoc power analysis was performed for the actual sample size (N = 142), comparing the power achieved with the minimum a priori sample size determined by G*Power analysis (n = 68). The power analysis confirmed that the statistical power for the study was sufficiently significant ($1 - \beta$) power of 0.99. For the post hoc power analysis, implications due to a small sample size are not included here since the sample size was above the minimum required.

Data Analysis Procedures

The Hayes PROCESS macro (Model 4) for simple mediation was used to estimate the mediation effects for all three research questions using OLS regression analysis. The PROCESS macro calculates path coefficients for direct and total effects and uses 5,000 bootstrap samples to produce confidence intervals for the indirect effects. These confidence intervals test whether trust in leaders mediates the relationship between servant leadership and the IT project success dimensions of project management success, perception success, and result success. The data analysis procedure for all three questions is described below, as the same process applies to each OLS regression analysis.

The OLS regression data analysis procedure aligns with the research questions and related hypotheses in several ways. First, the data was collected and reviewed to ensure no missing or erroneous values. Text-based responses were numerically coded and recoded in alignment with the quantitative methodology. The aggregated data was then processed per the instrument scoring guidelines. Assumption tests were conducted for all seven regression paths to assess that the data met OLS regression requirements. No data points were removed due to outliers, and all assumptions were met, suggesting the data were suitable for inferential analysis. Furthermore, reliability testing was conducted using Cronbach's alpha, where all instruments demonstrated values greater than 0.70 (ranging from .803 to .862), indicating acceptable reliability for this study. Lastly, a post hoc G*Power analysis (see Figure 10 in Appendix F) confirmed that the study had high statistical power (.99) due to the larger sample size.

The Hayes (2018) PROCESS macro was installed in SPSS v29 to conduct mediation analysis for all three research questions. The cleaned dataset was uploaded into SPSS, and model 4 of the PROCESS macro was selected, as recommended for simple mediation analysis (Klompstra et al., 2022). For each research question, the independent variable (X), mediating variable (M), and dependent variable (Y) were specified in the model. Bootstrapping was set to 5,000 with a 95% confidence interval to test for mediation effects. The PROCESS macro produced total, direct, and indirect effect statistics, which were analyzed to find whether mediation was present.

For all three research questions, the analysis followed the mediation model procedures by Hayes (2018). This procedure is for the short-term dimension criterion variable of project management success (Y_1) for this case. This analysis began with an examination of the total effect (path c) to assess the direct relationship between the independent variable (X), servant leadership, and the dependent variable (Y_1), project management success. Next, the direct effect of the independent variable (X), servant leadership, on the mediator (M), trust in leaders, known as path a, was evaluated to determine whether the independent variable influenced the mediator. The effect of the mediator (M), trust in leaders, on the dependent variable (Y_1), project management success, referred to as path b, was then examined to assess whether the mediator had a significant relationship with the outcome variable. Lastly, the direct effect (path c') was assessed while controlling for the mediator to determine whether mediation was present.

The indirect effect ($a*b$) was analyzed using bootstrap confidence intervals to confirm mediation. Mediation was considered present if the confidence interval did not contain zero and the null hypobook was rejected. If the confidence interval contained zero, mediation was not supported, and the null hypobook failed to be rejected (Clement & Bradley-Garcia, 2022). This process was repeated for each of the three research questions, substituting the dependent variable (Y) accordingly to evaluate the mediation effect across all dimensions of IT project success, which included project management success (Y_1), perception success (Y_2), and result success (Y_3).

For all three research questions, none of the bootstrap confidence intervals included zero. Furthermore, in each PROCESS macro OLS regression analysis, trust in leaders partially mediates all three relationships between servant leadership and the IT project success dimensions of project management success, perception success, and result success.

Results

Presenting the Results

This section presents each research question and its findings using written details, tables, and visual models. A total of ($N = 142$) participants from IT project teams within the United States were included in the analysis. The results section will provide each research question and the null and alternative hypotheses. Results are presented with tables displaying OLS regression analysis outcomes, direct, indirect, and total effects, and their respective confidence intervals, calculated using the Hayes PROCESS macro v4.3.

Mediation analysis is conducted when a predictive relationship between the predictor (X), servant leadership, and the criterion variables ($Y_1 – Y_3$): project management success, perception success, and result success (Hayes, 2018). All three regression models were tested at an $\alpha < .05$ level of significance, showing significant predictive relationships displayed as the (c path) in the following mediation results paragraphs below. These predictive relationships confirmed conducting the mediation analyses. All data collected for servant leadership, trust in leaders, project management success, perception success, and result success were ordinal treated as interval data for analysis.

Research Question 1. This research question used the Hayes PROCESS macro v4.3 in SPSS v29 to determine if trust in leaders mediates the relationship between servant leadership and project management success.

RQ1: Does trust in leaders mediate the relationship between servant leadership and project management success?

$H1_0$: Trust in leaders does not significantly mediate the relationship between servant leadership and project management success.

$H1_a$: Trust in leaders does significantly mediate the relationship between servant leadership and project management success.

First, there is a significant predictive relationship between servant leadership and project management success (c path) ($\beta = .440$, $p < .001$). The results suggest that servant leadership significantly predicted trust in leaders (*a* path) ($\beta = .766$, $p < .001$). Additionally, servant leadership had a significant direct effect on project management success (*c'* path) ($\beta = .292$, $p < .001$). Furthermore, trust in leaders significantly predicted project management success (*b* path) ($\beta = .194$, $p = .004$). The indirect effect of servant leadership on project management success through trust in leaders was also significant (*a**b* path), ($\beta = .149$, 95% CI [.032, .264]). Since the 95% confidence interval does not include zero, this finding suggests a significant indirect effect, supporting partial mediation of trust in leaders on the relationship between servant leadership and project management success. Thus, the null hypobook was rejected. Table 9 presents the detailed mediation analysis results, while Figure 32 illustrates the mediation model for this research question below.

Table 9

Results of Mediation Analysis for Research Question #1

	M (Trust in Leaders)				*Y* (Project Management Success)			
Antecedent	*B*	*SE*	*p*	β	*B*	*SE*	*p*	β
X (Servant Leadership) *a*	.766	.049	< .001	.795	*c'* .292	.063	< .001	.454
M (Trust in Leaders)	-	-	-	-	*b* .194	.066	.004	.291
	$R^2 = .632$				$R^2 = .501$			
	$F(1, 140) = 240.945, p < .001$				$F(2, 139) = 48.256, p < .001$			

Figure 32

Mediation Model

for Research Question #1

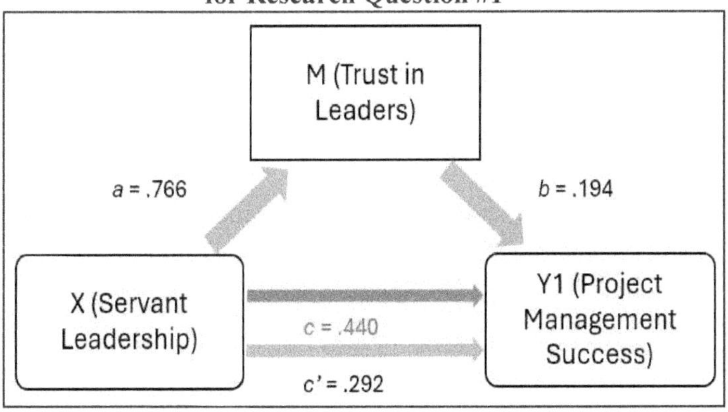

Research Question 2. This research question used the Hayes PROCESS macro v4.3 in SPSS v29 to determine if trust in leaders mediates the relationship between servant leadership and perception success.

RQ2: Does trust in leaders mediate the relationship between servant leadership and perception success?

$H2_0$: Trust in leaders does not significantly mediate the relationship between servant leadership and perception success.

$H2_a$: Trust in leaders does significantly mediate the relationship between servant leadership and perception success.

For the second research question, there is a significant predictive relationship between servant leadership and perception (c path) ($\beta = .434$, $p < .001$). The results indicated that servant leadership significantly predicted trust in leaders (*a* path) ($\beta = .766$, $p < .001$). Also, servant leadership significantly affected perception success (*c'* path) ($\beta = .241$, $p = .002$). Likewise, trust in leaders significantly predicted perception success (*b* path) ($\beta = .252$, $p = .002$). The indirect effect of servant leadership on perception success through trust in leaders was also significant (*a*b* path), ($\beta = .193$, 95% CI [.028, .347]). Because the 95% confidence interval does not include zero, this result supports a significant indirect effect, suggesting partial mediation of trust in leaders on the relationship between servant leadership and perception success. Hence, the null hypobook was rejected. Table 10 presents the detailed mediation analysis results, while

Figure 33 illustrates the mediation model for this research question below.

Table 10

Results of Mediation Analysis for Research Question #2

	M (Trust in Leaders)				*Y* (Project Management Success)			
Antecedent	*B*	*SE*	*p*	β	*B*	*SE*	*p*	β
X (Servant Leadership) *a*	.766	.049	< .001	.795	c' .241	.077	.002	.337
M (Trust in Leaders)	-	-	-	-	b .252	.080	.002	.339
	$R^2 = .632$				$R^2 = .410$			
	$F(1, 140) = 240.945, p < .001$				$F(2, 139) = 48.256, p < .001$			

Figure 33

for Research Question #2

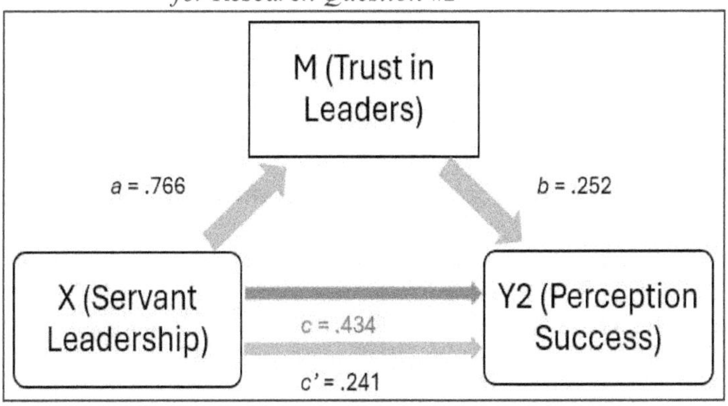

Research Question 3. Research Question 3 used the Hayes PROCESS macro v4.3 in SPSS v29 to determine if trust in leaders mediates the relationship between servant leadership and result success.

RQ3: Does trust in leaders mediate the relationship between servant leadership and result success?

H3$_0$: Trust in leaders does not significantly mediate the relationship between servant leadership and result success.

H3$_a$: Trust in leaders does significantly mediate the relationship between servant leadership and result success.

For the third research question, there is a significant predictive relationship between servant leadership and result success (c path) ($\beta = .404$, $p < .001$). As previously found, servant leadership significantly predicted trust in leaders (*a* path) ($\beta = .766$, $p < .001$). Moreover, servant leadership significantly affected result success (*c'* path) ($\beta =$ .220, $p = .002$). Furthermore, trust in leaders significantly predicted result success (*b* path), ($\beta = .240$, $p = .001$). The indirect effect of servant leadership on result success through trust in leaders was also significant (*a*b* path), ($\beta = .184$, 95% CI [.047, .317]). The 95% confidence interval does not include zero, confirming a significant indirect effect. This result indicates that trust in leaders partially mediates the relationship between servant leadership and result success. Therefore, the null hypobook was rejected. Table 11 presents the detailed results of the mediation analysis, while Figure 34 illustrates the mediation model for this research question below.

Table 11

Results of Mediation Analysis for Research Question #3

	M (Trust in Leaders)				*Y* (Project Management Success)			
Antecedent	*B*	*SE*	*p*	β	*B*	*SE*	*p*	β

X (Servant Leadership)	*a*	.766	.049	< .001	.795	c’	.220	.069	.002	.337
M (Trust in Leaders)		-	-	-	-	b	.240	.072	.001	.355
			$R^2 = .632$					$R^2 = .430$		
		$F(1, 140) = 240.945, p < .001$					$F(2, 139) = 52.405, p < .001$			

Figure 34

for Research Question #3

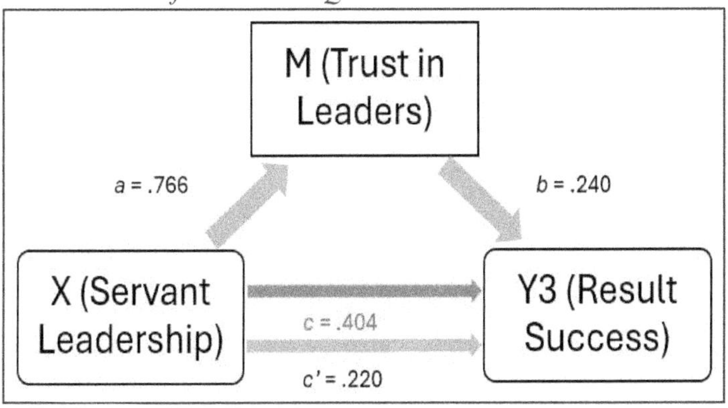

Limitations

Limitations are inherent in all research. According to Clarke et al. (2024), researchers can mitigate misinterpretations of findings by openly acknowledging their work's limitations. The following limitations affected the strength of this study's findings and highlight opportunities for future research to address these constraints, which will be discussed further in Chapter 5.

1. Participant responses were self-assessments, which may introduce selfreporting bias due to misinterpretation of survey items or inflating or skewing data toward leaders or themselves. This limitation was anticipated in Chapter 1 and presented during analysis showing responses clustering near the upper end of the scales for both servant

leadership and trust in leaders. Several items also showed minimal variance, and several respondents appeared to answer consistently across all items, which may indicate uniform response behavior. Misinterpretation of survey items or participant biases may result in the overestimation or underestimation of responses. Therefore, this limitation makes it more difficult to accurately determine the effects of servant leadership and trust in leaders on IT project success dimensions.

2. This study employed a cross-sectional design, capturing data at a single point in time. This design limitation remained consistent with expectations. However, during analysis, the single timepoint limited the ability to explore how trust and servant leadership may change across a project's lifecycle. As a result, the design restricted causal interpretation and made it more difficult to understand potential timing effects between predictor and outcome variables. As a result, it does not account for longitudinal differences and cannot establish causal relationships between variables.

3. This study used convenience sampling, which, while relevant to IT and ecommerce sectors, limits generalizability due to its non-random selection process. This limitation could be due to the sample not being fully representative of all IT project team members and industry sectors in the United States. Additionally, this limitation extends to not representing global IT project team members or other relevant industries.

4. A final limitation is that the IT project success model dimensions included only three Likert-scale items for project management success, a two-item scale for perception success, and a two-item scale for result success. he limited number of Likert-scale items may affect measurement validity and reliability. The two-item subscales provided limited measurement. The short length of these subscales reduced the ability to evaluate internal consistency and potentially limited the interpretation regarding how leadership influences perceived success. These limitations are the same as the anticipated limitations found in Chapter 1 of this research. However, the degree to which each limitation had effects on the study, such as self-reporting bias and scale limitations, presented more strongly than expected. While the sampling frame and crosssectional design limitations were consistent

with initial expectations. These limitations provide important context for understanding the study's findings and offer opportunities to refine future research. These limitations outline potential study constraints, potential impacts to reliability, and highlight opportunities for future research to explore these challenges.

Summary

This study examined whether trust in leaders mediates the relationship between servant leadership and IT project success dimensions of project management success, perception success, and result success. Data were collected from (N=142) IT project team members in the United States through paid Qualtrics© panel surveys, using validated Likert-scale instruments. The data was estimated using three OLS regression analyses using the Hayes PROCESS macro v4.3 to determine the mediation effects presented in the research questions. Several potential outlier cases were carefully evaluated using Cook's distance and leverage values to justify their inclusion in the final dataset. All assumption tests for the OLS regressions were met. Inferential analysis was suitable since the assumptions for linearity, heteroscedasticity, outliers, normality, and the absence of multicollinearity were met.

The findings demonstrate a significant predictive relationship between servant leadership and all three IT project success dimensions. For research question 1, the analysis determined that trust in leaders partially mediated the relationship between servant leadership and project management success. The calculated indirect effect (*a**b* path) was significant ($\beta = .149$, 95% CI [.032, .264]), confirming partial mediation. Likewise, for research question 2, trust in leaders partially mediates the relationship between servant leadership and perception success, with a significant indirect effect ($\beta = .193$, 95% CI [.028, .347]). Finally, for research question 3, trust in leaders also partially mediated the relationship between servant leadership and result success, with a significant indirect effect ($\beta = .184$, 95% CI [.047, .317]). Therefore, since the confidence intervals for all indirect effect paths did not include zero, the null hypotheses were rejected for all three research questions. While these findings were significant, the study's limitations also influenced these results.

Several limitations emerged that may have influenced the interpretation of these results. First, self-reported responses may have introduced response bias due to potential misinterpretation of the survey questions, which could skew data by overinflating or underinflating responses. Second, this study is cross-sectional, which prevented causal relationships from being determined between the variables. Third, convenience sampling limited the generalizability of findings beyond the IT and e-commerce sectors in the United States, as the sample may not fully represent all IT project team members across different industries. Moreover, this study was only conducted in the United States and is not generalizable to other cultures or global IT project teams. Lastly, the three IT project success dimensions relied on a limited number of items in each of the measurement scales used for inferential analysis, which could impact the reliability of the findings.

These results provide empirical evidence on the importance of trust in leaders in enhancing IT project success through servant leadership. These findings contribute to understanding leadership dynamics within IT project teams and indicate the need for that future research to refine leadership models and measurement approaches. Chapter 5 discusses the implications of these findings, the theoretical and practical applications for IT project leadership, the strengths and weaknesses of this research, and recommendations for future research and practice.

Chapter 5: Summary, Conclusions, and Recommendations

Introduction and Summary of Study

This research aimed to determine if trust in leaders mediates the relationship between servant leadership and the IT project success dimensions of project management success, perception success, and result success within IT project teams in the United States. The problem space for this study was centered on the topic of servant leadership and project success. Historical research found leadership style to be a significant factor in successful project outcomes (Anantatmula, 2010; Turner & Müller, 2005). Prior research indicates that servant leadership positively influences both general project success (Gwaya et al., 2014) and IT project success (Harwardt, 2018, 2020). However, most studies examining servant leadership and project success have been conducted in Pakistan (Bilal et al., 2021; Malik et al., 2022; Nauman et al., 2023). Moreover, servant leadership's effects on project success have been explored in the construction and NGO sectors
(Hassan et al., 2021; Mozammel & Abdulla, 2024; Nauman et al., 2023).

While the current book has demonstrated the mediating role of trust in leaders in construction projects (Hassan et al., 2021; Nauman et al., 2023), these studies were conducted outside the United States. Additionally, the current book also provided further recommendations to improve generalizability (Ellahi et al., 2022), provide a more humanistic view, and further exploration of mediating variables (Harwardt, 2020; Malik et al., 2022), specifically trust in leaders (Nauman et al., 2022a) affecting the relationship between servant leadership and project success. These recommendations highlight a significant gap in the book, as no prior research has examined the IT industry in the United States. Given the persistent IT project failure rates exceeding 60% since 2020 (Schmidt, 2022), further research was warranted to examine the role of leadership and trust in IT project success. This study addresses these gaps by examining how trust in leaders mediates the relationship between servant leadership and IT project success dimensions in IT teams in the United States.

This quantitative correlational predictive study determined how trust in leaders influences the relationship between servant leadership and the IT project success dimensions of project management success, perception success, and result success. The paid Qualtrics© platform was used to collect data from IT project team members within the United States. The three valid and reliable instruments used to gather data were the servant leadership model (Liden et al., 2015), the trust in leaders model (Podsakoff et al., 1990), and the IT project success model (Harwardt, 2018).

The findings of this study provide theoretical, practical, and methodological contributions to book. This study contributes to the understanding of servant leadership theory, the trust in-leaders model, and IT project success frameworks.

Moreover, these results refine the understanding of servant leadership influences within IT project environments and outcomes. These findings inform practical servant leadership training programs, organizational improvements, and improved IT project management team strategies. Additionally, this study utilized current survey instruments within the unexplored IT industry within the United States. Furthermore, developing trust in leaders has been linked to improved team performance (Chuang et al., 2021), psychological empowerment (Raiz et al., 2023), and overall project success (Nauman et al., 2023). Encouraging IT project leaders to adopt servant leadership behaviors may improve team effectiveness, reduce project failure rates, and mitigate financial losses.

By applying these relationships to the U.S. IT industry, this study expands existing models of servant leadership, trust in leaders, and IT project success. This study underscores the importance of examining mediating effects, like trust in leaders, to better understand how leadership influences IT project outcomes. Also, the findings provide organizations with insights into creating and implementing leadership development programs to enhance IT project team performance, improve project success rates, and mitigate financial losses for organizations.

The remainder of Chapter 5 summarizes the results, conclusions, strengths, weaknesses, and implications for research and practice based on this study. Additionally, the chapter presents recommendations for future research and practices. Chapter 5 concludes with a holistic reflection on the study's problem space and how the findings contribute to existing book and its application to leadership and IT project management.

Summary of Findings and Conclusion

Overall Organization

This study examined whether trust in leaders mediates the relationship between servant leadership and IT project success in the United States. Chapter 4 presented the results of the mediation analyses for each research question. This section summarizes those findings, highlights how they compare with the existing book detailed in

Chapter 2, and discusses the significance of these findings within servant leadership and IT project management settings. Each research question organizes this summary. RQ1 addressed whether trust in leadership mediated the relationship between servant leadership and project management success;

RQ2 addressed perception success; RQ3 addressed result success. The Hayes PROCESS macro v4.3 was used to examine each research question and assess whether trust in leaders mediates the relationship between servant leadership and IT project success dimensions.

Research Question 1. Using an OLS regression, the analysis of the Hayes PROCESS macro confirmed a partial mediation of trust in leaders on the relationship between servant leadership and project management success. The direct effect or the predictive relationship between servant leadership and project management success (*c* path) was significant ($\beta = .440$, $p < .001$).

Additionally, servant leadership significantly predicted trust in leaders (*a* path) ($\beta = .766, p < .001$), while servant leadership (*c′* path) ($\beta = .292, p < .001$) and trust in leaders (*b* path) ($\beta = .194$, $p = .004$) both significantly influenced project management success. However, the aim of the study, looking at the mediating indirect effect (*a*b*), was found to be significant ($\beta = .149$, 95% CI [.032, .264]). In conclusion, the indirect effect indicated significant positive partial mediation.

Therefore, the null hypobook was rejected.

The results of this study align with previous studies showing that servant leadership has a positive impact on the NGO (Ahmadzai, 2024; Amuna et al., 2021; Little & Martens, 2024; Malik et al., 2022; Mombeuil et al., 2023) and construction (S. Ali et al., 2023; Hassan et al., 2021; Mozammel & Abdulla, 2024; Nauman et al., 2023).

Additionally, these findings match the studies conducted in Pakistan (S. Ali et al., 2023; Bilal et al., 2021; Ellahi et al., 2022; Malik et al., 2022; Nauman et al., 2023). In those studies, servant leaders who prioritized their team members' needs over their own had improvements in the success of projects. For IT project teams in the United States, servant leaders who use a trustbased approach may help improve project management practices, such as planning, executing, and maintaining project plans.

Research Question 2. Using an OLS regression, the analysis of the Hayes PROCESS macro confirmed a partial mediation of trust in leaders on the relationship between servant leadership and perception success. The predictive relationship, or the direct effect between servant leadership and perception success (*c* path), was significant ($\beta = .434, p < .001$). Moreover, servant leadership significantly predicted trust in leaders (*a* path) ($\beta = .766, p < .001$), while servant leadership (*c′* path) ($\beta = .241, p = .002$) and trust in leaders (*b* path) ($\beta = .252, p = .002$) both significantly influenced perception success. The indirect effect ($a*b$) was also significant ($\beta = .193$, 95% CI [.028,.347]). Because the 95% confidence interval did not include zero, the findings indicated significant positive partial mediation. Therefore, the null hypobook was rejected.

These results indicate a positive relationship between servant leadership and trust in leaders, which may influence perceptions of success. While attempting to compare current book on the medium-term view of project success, the only current research that reflects these positive findings on the benefits of project success on stakeholders, clients, and end-user perceptions is by Harwardt (2018, 2020), which was not mediated by trust in leaders. In comparison, the results of this study suggest that the relationship between servant leadership and medium-term perceptions of project success, including stakeholder satisfaction and end-user perceptions is mediated by trust in leaders. In this study, by applying servant leadership principles emphasizing team well-being, employee empowerment, and open communication, IT leaders can build trust to promote improved attitudes and experiences for their stakeholders, clients, and end-users.

Research Question 3. Using an OLS regression, the analysis of the Hayes PROCESS macro confirmed a partial mediation of trust in leaders on the relationship between servant leadership and result success. The direct effect between servant leadership and result success (*c* path) was significant ($\beta = .404, p < .001$). Servant leadership also predicted trust in leaders (*a* path) ($\beta = .766, p < .001$), while servant leadership (*c'* path) ($\beta = .220, p = .002$) and trust in leaders (*b* path) ($\beta = .240, p = .001$) each had significant statistical impacts on result success. The indirect effect ($a*b$) was also significant ($\beta = .184$, 95% CI [.047, .317]). Like the previous research questions, since the 95% confidence interval did not include zero, these findings indicated significant positive partial mediation. Therefore, the null hypobook was rejected.

According to Harwardt (2018), result success reflects a project's longterm financial or strategic benefits, making this perspective on lasting organizational gains especially relevant. Like the reflection and comparison to medium-term success book, Harwardt (2018, 2020) are the most current studies that have explored how servant leadership influences long-term impacts of project success on organizational and strategic benefits. However, neither study delved into whether trust in leaders mediated the relationship between servant leadership and IT project success dimensions. By looking at the long-term view and impacts on IT project teams and their organizational benefits in the United States, these results suggest that servant leaders that use a trust based approach have long-term positive effects on organizational financial and strategic benefits.

Conclusion. In conclusion, these findings show that trust in leaders partially mediates the relationship between servant leadership and the shortterm (project management success), medium-term (perception success), and long-term (result success) dimensions in IT project teams in the United States. By concluding the positive impact of servant leadership on IT project teams, this study aligns with research conducted in the

NGO (Ahmadzai, 2024; Amuna et al., 2021; Little & Martens, 2024; Malik et al., 2022;

Mombeuil et al., 2023) and construction industries (S. Ali et al., 2023; Hassan et al., 2021; Mozammel & Abdulla, 2024; Nauman et al., 2023). Additionally, these findings match the studies conducted in Pakistan (S. Ali et al., 2023; Bilal et al., 2021; Ellahi et al., 2022; Malik et al., 2022; Nauman et al., 2023). Furthermore, the results show that when servant leaders prioritize their IT project team members' needs while promoting trust, they can improve project management practices, shape more favorable perceptions of project success, and contribute to enduring organizational benefits. These conclusions reinforce the significance of servant leadership and trust in leaders, extending the understanding of how these factors positively impact project success outcomes.

Reflection on the Book Process

Throughout the book journey, I discovered that the initial step of identifying a feasible research topic and being able to frame it within existing book is imperative. Initially, I attempted to tackle the broad topic of servant leadership behaviors and their impact on IT project success. However, it was quickly realized that focusing on a narrower problem space would be more practical and effective for doctoral study. Learning how to develop and refine a problem space based on the current recommendations and limitations was also a necessary set of skills. Through the research courses, consistent book reading, and refining my academic research and writing skills, I was better equipped to evaluate articles and iteratively transform from a doctoral student into an academic researcher.

Designing the study also highlighted how expectations around collecting data can be different in reality. My expectations and reliance that large social media groups would provide enough participants was proven wrong. Moreover, having a large pool of potential participants in social media groups does not guarantee immediate or an abundant amount of responses. The failure to capture data through social media groups allowed me to understand another lesson in this doctoral process: to use a paid survey service, like Qualtrics© for this study. Paying for this service provided an efficient and effective way to collect data. Although the paid service route was the least cost-effective, it saved time and provided accurate data that aligned with the study's purpose and research question aims.

Another reflection on the doctoral transformation process is about conducting the data analysis. I had not previously performed any mediation analyses, and learning from Hayes's (2018) book on mediation and moderation improved my ability to interpret direct, indirect, and total effects. Initially, I struggled to decide which outputs to include and how to convey the findings. However, I finally understood what the mediation paths meant and how to interpret the results of the research questions. To build confidence was videos, mediation documentation, and support from previous students and current cohort members proved the most effective strategy. Additionally, several benefits stemmed from my experiences at the residencies at Grand Canyon University for doctoral students as part of the degree program. These benefits included allowing students to ask questions face-to-face with instructors, refining presentation skills, and fostering a better understanding of how each component of the research development aligns with the study's purpose, methodology, design, and type of analysis.

From an internal perspective, through this book process, I developed perseverance, dedication, consistency, and integrity. From an external point of view, mentorship, asking questions and staying engaged in scholarly book are essential. Grand Canyon University's approach of allowing students to explore the book process early on and collaborate with instructors, staff, and peers allowed me to find a relevant and feasible topic while also helping me to improve the study's frameworks and aims. The guidance I received helped me adjust my problem space and research questions to something more manageable, underscoring how openness to feedback offered a more feasible study. When reflecting on the doctoral experience, I am grateful for the supportive environment GCU provided. This support allowed me to develop as a researcher and provide a meaningful and rewarding book study that expanded academic knowledge, business insights, and enhanced the servant leadership and IT project management communities.

Implications

The purpose of this study was to determine if trust in leaders mediated the relationship between servant leadership and the IT project success dimensions in IT project teams in the United States.This section includes discussions on the theoretical, practical, and future implications based on the findings of this research. Centered on the servant leadership theory, the trust in leaders model, and the IT project success dimensions of project management success, perception success, and result success.

Theoretical Implications

This study applied servant leadership theory, originally introduced by Greenleaf (1970), using Liden et al.'s (2015) SL-7 model. The SL-7 emphasizes altruistic type behaviors such as emotional healing, empowering subordinates and putting followers first (Haq et al., 2022; Liden et al., 2015). Previous research has linked servant leadership to enhanced organizational citizenship behavior, improving the effectiveness and performance of individuals, organizations (Howladar & Rahman, 2021), and teams (Parris & Peachey, 2013). Additionally, prior research found that servant leadership significantly impacts team performance through different mediating and moderating mechanisms, such as team cohesion, team learning (Abdolmaleki & Ghanbari, 2021), team climate (Arshad et al., 2022), increased work engagement (Zhou et al., 2022), internal social capital, TMX (Ruiz-Palomino et al., 2023) and teamwork (Swanson et al., 2022). These prior findings align with those of this study as servant leadership was determined to have a significant direct effect on project management success (direct effect) (β =

.440, $p < .001$) and that relationship was partially mediated by trust in leaders

(indirect effect) (β = .149, 95% CI [.032, .264]). These results suggest that the influence of servant leadership on short-term project outcomes is partially explained by the level of trust IT project team members have in their leaders.

The Trust-in-Leaders model (Podsakoff et al., 1990) conceptualizes trust as followers' faith and loyalty in their leaders. Previous research shows that followers consider their leaders trustworthy when they see their leaders as having integrity, competence, and benevolence (Kim et al., 2004; Mayer et al., 1995). In this study, it was found that servant leadership significantly predicts perception success (direct effect) (β = .434, $p < .001$) and that trust in leaders mediates this relationship (indirect effect) (β = .193, 95% CI [.028, .347]). These findings support earlier research indicating that various leadership styles, such as ethical (Bhatti et al., 2021), humble (Hassan et al.,

2023), transformational (Fareed et al., 2022; Saeed et al., 2023), transactional, and laissez-faire (Khan et al., 2021), that leadership styles affect project success through the mediating variable of trust. This study fills the gap presented in the current book (Nauman et al., 2022b) by showing that trust explains how servant leadership behaviors lead to improved perceptions among IT team members. These results refine the trust-in-leaders (TIL) model for IT project contexts by demonstrating that the positive effects of servant leadership rely on the level of trust that followers have in their leaders.

Another theoretical implication is that the results of this research confirm that IT project success most comprehensively understood as a multidimensional construct. Unlike traditional success models such as the Iron Triangle (Atkinson, 1999), which focus solely on the project management practices of being on time, budget, and within scope, Harwardt's (2018) ITPS model presents a multidimensional framework by capturing short-term, medium-term, and long-term outcomes. By integrating short-, medium-, and long-term success, Harwardt's ITPS model not only addresses the limitations of the Iron Triangle but also provides a relevant framework for U.S. IT projects. In contrast to the ITPS model, the Zwikael and Meredith (2021) model is a generic multidimensional approach to project success. Moreover, the Zwikael and Meredith (2021) model was developed using perspectives from academics, industry experts, and business executives, whereas the ITPS model is the only model developed from the management perspective.

The ITPS model provides a management perspective that assesses short-, medium-, and long-term benefit time frames of IT projects. This study found a positive relationship between all three dimensions and servant leadership when partially mediated by trust in leaders. This integrated view of ITPS offers valuable insights into both theory and practice in the IT industry in the United States. Additionally, the ITPS framework is significant for the U.S. IT industry as the traditional Iron Triangle metrics do not holistically capture the medium-term stakeholder perspectives or the longterm strategic benefits to organizations. While there are theoretical implications with this research based on the frameworks and findings of the study, there are also practical implications for businesses and practitioners.

Practical Implications

As a result of this study, there are several implications for IT project managers, executives, and organizations that involve servant leadership values. This study confirmed that trust in leaders partially mediates the relationship between servant leadership and IT project success, aligning with prior research indicating that leadership style influences project outcomes (Turner & Müller, 2005). These results align with prior studies in the construction industry in Bahrain (Mozammel & Abdulla, 2024) and Pakistan (Hassan et al., 2021; Nauman et al., 2023), where servant leadership positively impacted project success through trust-building factors. However, this study extends the research into IT project environments in the United States, indicating that servant leadership improves project success by fostering trust in a technological setting within the United States.

Integrating servant leadership training and trust-building programs to improve project management effectiveness is a key implication for IT teams and organizations. Prior research emphasizes that trust improves project success (Bhatti et al., 2021; Majeed et al., 2021), team performance (Chuang et al., 2021), job satisfaction (Fareed et al., 2022), and project performance (Zhang & Li, 2024), and this study confirms that these dynamics also apply to IT project teams. Organizations can reduce IT project failure rates and improve stakeholder engagement by prioritizing servant leadership with trustbuilding characteristics, such as open communication and employee empowerment.

The findings also highlight the importance of stakeholder perceptions in IT project success. Previous studies suggested that servant leadership enhances employees' perception of leadership effectiveness through positive interactions that promote a trusting climate, improved work engagement (Rahal & Farmanesh, 2022; Zhou et al., 2022), and motivation, along with increased customer satisfaction (Qiu & Dooley, 2022), and this study extends those findings by demonstrating that trust in leaders improves the perception success dimension in IT projects. The alignment of prior research with this study suggests that to bolster stakeholder satisfaction and project success, IT leaders should regularly involve stakeholders, clarify project goals, and maintain communication.

Furthermore, this study contributes to understanding the long-term organizational benefits associated with servant leadership. While prior research established that servant leadership enhances strategic competitive advantages (Andry, 2023), business value (Pashutan et al., 2022), process improvements (Reich & Peppard, 2022), organizational agility, and sustainability (Zaleski & Michalski, 2021), this study demonstrates that these effects extend to IT project teams and organizations in the United States. Organizations that develop servant leaders and trust may experience sustained project success, improved business agility, and enhanced innovation, improving the long-term value of leadership development programs.

Future Research Implications

The results of this study also have significant implications for future research in leadership, trust, and IT project management. This study provides empirical evidence for trust in leaders as a partial mediator in the relationship between servant leadership and IT project success. Still, future studies could explore additional mediators and moderators that influence this relationship (Malik et al., 2022). One direction for future research is examining additional mediators beyond trust in leaders. While this study found trust to be a key explanation variable, other mediators such as team cohesion, team learning (Abdolmaleki & Ghanbari, 2021), team climate

(Arshad et al., 2022), work engagement (Zhou et al., 2022), internal social capital, TMX (Ruiz-Palomino et al., 2023) and teamwork (Swanson et al., 2022) may also impact IT project success. Future research could examine whether these factors moderate, mediate, or further explain how servant leadership influences IT project team structures, including in different cultural, regional, or global settings.

Additionally, longitudinal studies could provide insights into how trust in leaders evolves in IT project teams. Prior research has shown that organizational benefits such as cost savings, revenue generation (Jasmi et al., 2022), competitive advantage (Andry, 2023), performance enhancements (Pashutan et al., 2022; Reich & Peppard, 2022), increased agility, greater sustainability, and improved stakeholder engagement (Perera et al., 2023; Zaleski & Michalski, 2021). Therefore, conducting research examining the long-term view provides insights into the complexities and benefits that make up project success over a more extended period. This future research implication can further strengthen the result success dimension of the ITPS model. Additionally, longitudinal research could also help determine causality.

The last future research implication could be to explore the impact of emerging technologies and remote work on servant leadership effectiveness. As IT teams increasingly move to virtual and hybrid work environments, it is essential to understand how servant leaders build trust in the IoT space. Prior studies suggest that positive servant leadership interactions improve work engagement (Rahal & Farmanesh, 2022) and employee self-efficacy (Isabel et al., 2023) to help create trust (Little & Martens, 2024). However, with the rise of AI-driven project management tools, future research implications of this study could investigate how trust and leadership styles can be adapted to virtual IT teams.

Strengths and Weaknesses of the Study

Strengths of the Study. One of the strengths of this research is that it relies on valid and reliable theoretical foundations. This study used three models and theories aligned with IT project success to ensure consistency with prior research. This study examined the relationship between leadership, trust, and project outcomes using the servant leadership (SL-7) model (Liden et al., 2015), the trust in leaders (TIL) model (Podsakoff et al., 1990), and the IT project success (Harwardt, 2018). By using Hayes' PROCESS Model 4 (Hayes, 2018), the study strengthens its contribution by identifying the role of TIL in explaining the relationship between SL and IT project success. The use of OLS regression analysis further strengthens the study's contribution to leadership and IT project management research.

Another strength of this study is that the minimum recommended sample size, or a prior sample size, was sufficiently large and powerful for this mediation analysis. Ensuring there are enough participant responses enhances the statistical power of the findings. This statistical power allows for significant statistical testing of the direct and indirect effects. When there is a larger sample size in mediation analysis, there is a reduction in the risk of biases, which increases the reliability of the study findings.

The last strength of this study is that the findings provide practical implications for IT project leadership. The findings foster meaningful understanding for IT project managers, as the results found that TIL is vital in enhancing the success of projects when servant leadership is present. Moreover, organizations can extend these findings into leadership and team training programs to foster trust and improve project performance. Therefore, by presenting the significance of follower trust in IT project team members, the study contributes to servant leadership development strategies and advises future management practices.

Weaknesses of the Study. Despite the strengths of this study, there are several weaknesses that limit and weaken the generalizability and interpretability of its findings. The first primary limitation is the use of a cross-sectional design, which only collects data from a single point in time. This design has a limit to the ability to prove causal inferences. For this study, this limitation prevents conclusions about whether SL directly influences TIL, which subsequently impacts IT project success. A longitudinal study would be required to understand how variables cause findings over time to determine causal inferences.

Another weakness, based on the limitations, is the use of the correlational predictive design does not establish causality. This means that although significant relationships were found in this study, additional causal explanations cannot be ruled out. Additional variables, such as organizational strategies, industry sector, or regional cultures, could also influence IT project success. Therefore, a structural equation modeling design could provide the required data for causal inferences.

A third weakness is the use of convenience sampling. This sampling approach may introduce bias and limit the generalizability of the findings. The non-random sampling approach means that the sample may not fully represent IT project teams across all industry sectors in the United States. Additionally, self-selection bias risk is introduced when survey participation is voluntary, as respondents may skew the results of the study due to participants potentially having significant investments in the findings of servant leadership effectiveness and project performance outcomes. This bias could inflate or deflate the significance of the results. The use of randomized sampling in future studies would mitigate self-selection bias.

The last weakness of the study is the limited measurement scales for the IT project success dimensions. The project management success dimension used only three

Likert-scale items, while perception success and result success relied on twoitem scales. The weaknesses and limitations extend from these scales, such as not being able to appropriately measure IT project success, potentially influencing the reliability of the study findings. Therefore, future research should use or create and validate additional multi-scale models that could provide a more comprehensive assessment of the IT project success dimensions.

Recommendations

The following recommendation sections comprises four avenues of further research and four for future practice that are based on the results of this study on whether trust in leaders mediates the relationship between servant leadership and the IT project success dimensions of project management success, perception success, and result success in IT project teams in the United States. This research addressed gaps in understanding servant leadership within the U.S. IT industry by examining trust in leaders as a mediating variable on the existing predictive relationship between the predictor variable of servant leadership and the three criterion variables of the

IT project success model. The current study found trust in leaders to significantly partially mediate all three predictive relationships based on the three criterion variables.

Recommendations for Future Research

First, future research should conduct longitudinal studies to examine how trust in leaders influences IT project success over time. This study utilized a cross-sectional design, which captures relationships at a single point in time but does not account for how trust may develop and impact project outcomes across different project benefit phases. A longitudinal approach could provide additional insights into how trust in leaders evolves and affects IT project performance throughout project lifecycles. Additionally, a longitudinal study could offer the ability to determine causal inferences.

Second, expanding the study to other industries and geographical regions would enhance the generalizability of the findings. This study focused on IT project teams in the United States, yet existing book highlights that servant leadership and trust dynamics may vary across industries and cultural contexts. Researchers could conduct studies examining servant leadership and trust in leaders within different sectors in the United States, such as construction, healthcare, banking, education, or governmental industries. Additionally, research could be conducted by extending this study into diverse international settings.

The third future research recommendation is that qualitative research is needed to understand better how IT project team members perceive and experience trust in servant leaders. While this study quantitatively measured trust in leaders and its mediation effect, qualitative methods such as interviews or focus groups could provide rich insights into how servant leadership fosters trust and enhances IT project outcomes.

The fourth future research recommendation is that future studies should investigate additional mediating and moderating variables that may influence the relationship between servant leadership and IT project success. While this study identified trust in leaders as a mediating variable, future research could explore additional mediators such as team cohesion, team learning, team climate, work engagement, internal social capital, TMX, and team potency to further clarify how servant leadership influences project outcomes. Moreover, research conducted using moderators, such as organizational culture or leadership tenure, may also reveal results in which servant leadership is most effective.

Future research should refine and expand measurement models for IT project success dimensions to enhance validity and reliability in this field. This study utilized the IT project success model (Harwardt, 2018), which includes project management success, perception success, and result success. Additional research should refine and validate these measures or consider including new success dimensions to assess IT project performance further.

Recommendations for Future Practice

First, organizations should integrate servant leadership principles into leadership development programs. Since servant leadership was found to significantly impact IT project success, leadership training should emphasize behaviors such as ethical conduct, empowerment, and fostering trust. Organizations can implement coaching and mentoring training programs and workshops that develop servant leadership competencies among project managers, factors that also build trust. Additionally, organizations could implement feedback mechanisms, such as one-on-one meetings and employee surveys, to assess trust levels within IT project teams.

The second recommendation for future practice is that project management settings and teams should integrate trust-building and servant leadership principles. IT project methodologies such as Agile or Scrum could benefit from incorporating servant leadership strategies that enhance team collaboration, motivation, and performance. Organizations should encourage project managers to adopt the servant leadership style, which promotes employee growth and fosters a trusting climate.

The last future practice recommendation is that organizations should implement strategies for improving IT project outcomes through the servant leadership approach. Since this study found that the variables of servant leadership and trust in leaders have positive impacts on IT project success, firms should develop policies and procedures that promote these altruistic characteristics. By providing servant leadership training specific to IT project managers, formal trust-building training can contribute to improved IT project success rates.

Holistic Reflection on the Problem Space

This study addressed a gap in the book by exploring how trust in leaders mediates the relationship between servant leadership and IT project success dimensions of project management success, perception success, and result success in IT project teams within the United States. Prior research established that servant leadership positively impacts project success in industries such as NGOs (Ahmadzai, 2024; Amuna et al.,

2021; Malik et al., 2022; Mombeuil et al., 2023) or construction firms (S. Ali et al., 2023; Jan, 2025; Khalil et al., 2025; Nauman et al., 2023). However, it was not known how the servant leadership approach influenced IT project teams in the United States. Additionally, while prior studies had identified trust as a crucial mediating factor of servant leadership and project success (Hassan et al., 2021; Jan, 2025; Mozammel & Abdulla, 2024; Nauman et al., 2023), no research had examined trust in leaders as a mediating variable in the relationship between servant leadership and the IT project success dimensions. This study addresses this gap by demonstrating that trust in leaders partially mediates the existing predictive relationship between servant leadership and the IT project success dimensions of short-term (project management success), medium-term (perception success), and long-term (result success) in the IT industry within the United States.

Additionally, the findings of this study indicated that servant leadership is positively associated with IT project success, reinforcing its relevance as a leadership approach in these settings. Moreover, trust in leaders emerged as a crucial factor through which servant leadership impacts these three IT project time frame benefits. Furthermore, servant leaders who establish a trusting climate can enhance project management practices, improve stakeholder perceptions, and contribute to long-term organizational benefits. Also, these findings contribute to theoretical and practical understandings of servant leadership in IT project management. The study further validated the utilization of the IT project success model (Harwardt, 2018) within the U.S. IT sector by strengthening its relevance for evaluating the success of IT projects.

This study contributes to academic book by offering significant implications for business and project management leaders. IT project failures remain an issue, with over 60% of projects in the United States failing since 2020 (L. Ali et al., 2023). Additionally, this study provided evidence to support bringing servant leadership principles into IT project management settings. Moreover, the evidence provided in this study fosters a strategic approach for organizations to enhance leadership effectiveness. In conclusion, by fostering trust among team members, IT leaders may contribute to more successful project outcomes, increase team cohesion, and reduced risks associated with high project failure rates.